P9-APT-522

UNDERSTANDING
FINANCIAL INFORMATION
The non-financial manager's guide

Michael M. Coltman, M.B.A.

Self-Counsel Press Inc.
a subsidiary of
International Self-Counsel Press Ltd.
Canada   U.S.A.
(Printed in Canada)

Printed in Canada

First edition: December, 1982; Reprinted: October, 1988
Second edition: July, 1990

Canadian Cataloguing in Publication Data

Coltman, Michael M. (Michael Macdonald), 1930-
    Understanding financial information

    (Self-counsel business series)
    Previously published as: Financial control for the small business.
    ISBN 0-88908-928-0

    1. Small business — Finance.   2. Accounting.
I. Title.   II. Title: Financial control for the small business.
III. Series.
HG4027.7.C64 1990   658.15'92   C90-091273-1

Self-Counsel Press Inc.
a subsidiary of
International Self-Counsel Press Ltd.
Head and Editorial Office
1481 Charlotte Street
North Vancouver, British Columbia
Canada V7J 1H1

U.S. Address
1704 N. State Street
Bellingham, Washington 98225

CONTENTS

LIST OF SAMPLES

LIST OF TABLES

1

INTRODUCTION

Entrepreneurship and small business are not new to the U.S. Several hundred years ago the small business operator was thriving in this country in the form of the fur trapper and the homesteader, many of whom traded with larger companies (the monopolists of their day).

Not much has changed. Today large companies still tend to monopolize many markets, but small businesses nevertheless continue to thrive and grow by filling a niche that large companies cannot handle.

a. OPPORTUNITIES FOR SMALL BUSINESS

Most businesses that are large today began as small businesses. They became large because they were well managed and took advantage of opportunities that still exist. Today, small businesses can start up and, given the right circumstances, can grow. Some of these opportunities are:

(a) Trying out new ideas or products

(b) Offering personal services where the visibility and attention of the business owner is important such as in a restaurant, a beauty parlor, or an equipment repair firm

(c) Reaching a limited market, such as a grocery store that does not compete with a supermarket chain but offers necessary products when the chain stores are closed, or provides faster service since lines at cashier stations are avoided.

(d) Reaching a local market. A local small construction firm in a growing small town does not normally have to fear the competition of the large city construction companies who need the big economies of scale to survive.

(e) Catering to seasonal demands by being able to quickly adjust production to changing demands. Large manufacturing companies, for example, can not retool quickly in the short run. They need large stable markets and the manufacture of large quantities of products in order to remain profitable.

1. Adaptability of small business

Large corporations, because of their size and financial power, are frequently able to avoid the competition that small businesses face. A small business survives because it is much more adaptable and, therefore, more efficient than a huge corporate enterprise. Decision making is immediate and effective in a small business but slow, cumbersome, and often irrational in a large conglomerate where committees, rather than a down-to-earth sense or feeling about the market place, dictate decisions.

This adaptability is illustrated by the employment record of small businesses in the past 10 years. During this period an estimated five million new firms have been started (unfortunately not all of them have survived), and they have provided approximately 85% of all new jobs created in the country during this period. At the same time employment in larger firms, many of them in manufacturing, has declined, as these firms reacted slowly to the changing demand for their products and they have been less able to compete with foreign manufacturers.

b. SMALL BUSINESS DEFINITION

What is a small business? Definitions abound, but many of them are meaningless, particularly when expressed in terms of annual sales dollars, or number of persons employed. Perhaps the best description is that of the U.S. Congress' Small Business Act of 1934, which defines a small business as one "which is independently owned and operated and not dominant in its field."

It is estimated that there are more than 10.5 million non-farm businesses (out of about 11 million in total) in the U.S. that fit this definition. Most of them are labor intensive and provide employment opportunities far in excess of their relative size.

Most of these small companies were established to manufacture, distribute, and retail an inordinate variety of goods and services to both U.S. citizens and residents of other countries. Despite the fact that the large corporations receive much publicity, most large companies are dependent on small business. For example, companies that mass produce manufactured goods could not possibly distribute them without the myriad of small firms that handle transportation, wholesaling, and retailing. In other words, small business enterprises constitute the backbone of free enterprise economies like that of the U.S.

c. SKILLS REQUIRED

Traditionally, the level of management skills has been considerably less in small businesses than in larger ones, but the market that these small businesses face is just as complex as that to which large corporations are exposed.

The small business entrepreneur needs basically the same management skills as managers in a large business. They both must plan, make decisions based on the best information available, and prepare strategies for the future.

The small business owner/manager must make constant decisions to solve problems, resolve priorities, determine policies, make financial decisions and so on. In addition, operating results must be constantly analyzed, and outside factors that may have an effect on the internal operations of the business must be considered.

The individual small business owner must, however, assume a wider range of responsibilities than the general manager of a large corporation. The manager of a large corporation will have vice-presidents for finance, for marketing, for manufacturing and production, for distribution, and so on. Each of these vice-presidents has important responsibilities, but each is concerned with only one specific area of the company's activities.

In the small business, the owner generally has a daily responsibility for all of the above as well as for ongoing problems concerning personnel, inventory, sales, credit, suppliers, new policy implementation, new product introductions, public relations, marketing, and financial reporting.

However, it is difficult for the small business entrepreneur to copy the skills required for large businesses since these skills need to be adapted and scaled down. Unfortunately, most of the business books and material written to help businesses and managers survive are written for the large, corporate enterprise. This one is not.

d. RISK INVOLVED

Those who go into small business do so in spite of, or in ignorance of, the skills required and the odds for survival. A rule of thumb for new small businesses is that 50% fail during the first year, and 90% fail in less than five years.

Statistical analysis of business failures in the U.S. shows that the following causes make up more than 95% of the failures:

(a) Lack of competence to run the business
(b) Lack of experience in that type of business
(c) Lack of managerial experience
(d) Unbalanced experience

In addition, small business failures are said to be caused by any or all of the following specific problems:

(a) Inability to find competent employees
(b) Inadequate starting capital
(c) Inability to finance expansion
(d) Inadequate sales because of lack of demand for the product or service
(e) High operating expenses
(f) Limited credit from suppliers
(g) Shortage of working capital

(h) Poor location

(i) Inability to make a new product known to the market

(j) Impossible tax burdens

(k) Failure to formulate and plan objectives

(l) Pressure from large competitors with a vested interest to see the business fail

(m)Inability to keep proper accounting records

You will notice that many of the items mentioned in the above list relate to financial factors. In fact, most aspects of a business are eventually reflected in one way or another in the financial statements. The small business owner's ability to interpret, analyze, and make decisions about the information presented by the financial statements and related financial information is what this book is all about.

2

AN OVERVIEW OF ACCOUNTING

Owners of small businesses often react to accounting in horror, with visions of spending "accountless" hours on journals, ledgers and other mysterious accounting records. Because of the apparent mystery surrounding accounting, many small firm owners fail to keep adequate records and make no attempt to understand the basics of accounting. As a result, they often do not know whether the business made a profit or a loss until weeks after the end of their fiscal year simply because their accountant has not had time to prepare proper financial statements.

Although "official" financial statements are important and necessary in such matters as filing income tax returns, there is no reason why the owner of any small business, given adequate accounting records, cannot prepare interim financial statements that will give at least some indication of how the business is faring on an annual or, preferably, a monthly basis.

You don't have to be an accountant to do this. (And your accountant wouldn't want you to be one since he or she wants to stay in business too.) All you need is a basic understanding of the process and language of accounting. With this and the help of your accountant to set up some simple accounting records, you can do much of the basic bookkeeping work yourself and even prepare preliminary financial statements.

a. BASIC ACCOUNTING INFORMATION
Any business needs to have a record of some basic information.

1. Sales
Sales (sometimes called revenue) should be recorded by the day, week, month, or quarter, then further broken down

into cash or credit (by type of credit card if necessary), and by department, type of merchandise, or kind of product.

Credit sales are necessary in order to determine the amount of accounts receivable (money owed to you) at any particular time. Electronic registers can readily provide much of the required detail concerning sales without requiring extensive paperwork.

2. Operating expenses

Operating expenses should be recorded by type (for example purchases, supplies, rent) in total by sales period, and even by department, or type of merchandise or product. In a manufacturing company, expenses are often broken down into departments such as manufacturing, selling, and administration. In addition, unpaid expenses at any time need to be known since these form your accounts payable.

3. Payroll

This is a major expense for most firms and one that has legal requirements concerning the detail that you must record. In particular, payroll withholdings for taxes and FICA contributions under the Federal Insurance Contributions Act for health and welfare, disability, and pension benefits for employees must be properly documented.

4. Inventory

Inventory should be taken at least annually and, in certain businesses, as frequently as monthly. Inventory must be separated by type, and even by item. Electronic sales registers can often be used to record reductions in inventory as a result of a sale.

For all sales and expenses it is important that you keep all documents supporting any transactions such as sales slips, register tapes, or invoices; purchase invoices and/or receiving reports; cancelled checks for both operating expenses and payroll; and receipts or memos for cash pay outs not otherwise supported by an invoice or check.

b. THE BALANCE SHEET EQUATION

Accounting was developed to identify and record financial information about a business. It provides information about your company's assets and debts, your investment, sales (revenue), and expenses. It permits you or your accountant to prepare, in addition to the basic financial statements (balance sheet and income statement), other financial reports and analyses that will help you in making decisions and in running an efficient, effective business.

In every business, a set of financial statements is prepared periodically to monitor the progress of the business. The basic documents in this set of financial statements are an income statement and a balance sheet — both of which will be discussed in more detail in the next chapter.

The income statement shows the revenues (sales) less the expenses to arrive at net income. The net income (or loss, if expenses exceed revenues) is transferred to the balance sheet and becomes part of the owners' equity. If all entries for transactions have been made correctly the balance sheet will then "balance." The balance sheet equation is: Assets = liabilities + owners' equity.

Assets are things owned by your business (e.g., cash, inventory, building). Liabilities are items owed by your business (e.g. debts or obligations, including unpaid accounts, bank loans, or a mortgage on the building).

Owners' equity (also sometimes referred to as "net worth") is the difference between the assets and the liabilities. It is comprised of the money that you and any other owners have invested in the business, plus the profits of the business, less any losses, since the business began.

It perhaps makes more sense, from an owner's perspective, to state the balance sheet equation as: Assets - liabilities = owners' equity. That would be the case if the business were sold or liquidated. In other words, the assets would be sold off, the liabilities paid off, and the owner(s) would receive whatever was left. However, logical as this view of the balance sheet is, accountants prefer to express the equation in the traditional way since an even "balance" is then maintained.

c. TRANSACTIONS

A business transaction is an exchange of goods or services (e.g., the sale of an item in a retail store). In accounting, each transaction affects two or more accounts. This is why it is frequently referred to as double-entry accounting. No transaction can affect only one account. In this way, the balance sheet is always kept in balance and your accountant is eternally happy. Every transaction causes increases and/or decreases in asset and/or liability and/or owners' equity accounts.

This is illustrated very simply. Suppose you start a new retail business by investing $25,000 of your own savings in shares of the new company. The balance sheet would look like this:

ASSETS	OWNER'S EQUITY
Cash: $25,000	Shares: $25,000

Then you purchase $5 000 of goods on credit from a wholesaler so that you will have an inventory of goods on hand to sell in your retail store. The balance sheet would now look like this:

ASSETS		LIABILITY	
Cash:	$25,000	Accounts payable:	$ 5,000
Inventory:	$ 5,000		
		OWNER'S EQUITY	
		Shares:	$25,000
TOTALS:	$30,000		$30,000

The balance sheet still balances since the left-hand side (totalling $30,000) equals the right-hand side (also totalling $30,000). In normal practice, transactions like this are not recorded directly onto the balance sheet (since the balance sheet just wouldn't have enough room on it). They are entered into accounting records called journals and then into accounts in a ledger, or directly into the accounts in the ledger. It is the ledger, supported by the journals, that is commonly called the "books of account."

d. ACCOUNTS

There is usually one account in the ledger for each type of asset, liability, owners' equity, sale (revenue), and expense. At the end of each accounting period only the account balances at that time are transferred either to the balance sheet, or to the income statement. The income statement details all the income and expense accounts that comprise the owners' equity account on the balance sheet.

In accounting, each account is considered to have a left-hand side and a right-hand side. The left-hand side is where debit (usually abreviated to Dr) entries are made, and the right-hand side is where credit (Cr) entries are made:

Debit (Dr)	Credit (Cr)

Because of their shape, these accounts are referred to as "T" accounts. In practice you will never see accounts that look like this but they are a very useful learning device.

Account pages in ledgers are a bit more sophisticated; nevertheless, even with computer produced accounts and financial statements, the same basic principle of debits and credits applies.

When you enter transactions in the accounts, make sure the entries in the debit side of the accounts always equal the entries in the credit side. If you don't, the balance sheet will not balance. At the end of each accounting period, as the accounts are closed, the difference between the debit and credit entries provides the balance figure for each account.

It is wrong to view debits as increases and credits as decreases in the balance of accounts. Debits or credits can either increase or decrease the balance. These rules are illustrated in the following "T" accounts:

ASSETS		=	LIABILITIES		+	OWNERS' EQUITY	
Debits increase balance	Credits decrease balance		Debits decrease balance	Credits increase balance		Debits decrease balance	Credits increase balance

Since sales revenue (income) increases owners' equity, sales account entries have the same effect as those for the owners' equity account, and since expenses decrease owners' equity, expense account entries are the reverse of those for sales. This is illustrated by the following:

SALES		EXPENSES	
Debits decrease balance	Credits increase balance	Debits increase balance	Credits decrease balance

The normal account balance for each of the five types of accounts would be:

ACCOUNT	NORMAL BALANCE
Asset	Debit
Liability	Credit
Owners' equity	Credit
Sales	Credit
Expenses	Debit

and an example of each would be:

Asset:

Cash

12,000	

Liability:

Accounts Payable

	5,000

Owners' equity:

Shares

	8,000

Sales:

Sales revenue

	30,000

Expense:

Wages

6,000	

e. MATCHING PRINCIPLE

An important concept in accounting is the matching principle. The matching principle states that transactions are recorded at the time they occur and not necessarily at the time cash is exchanged. In other words, a regular customer may be allowed to charge a purchase to an account that is sent after the end of the month. Under the matching principle, the sale would be shown as revenue for the month even though the cash may not be received for another month.

This matching is known as accrual accounting, as opposed to cash accounting under which entries are made in the books only when cash is received or given out.

This does not suggest that cash basis accounting should never be used. In fact, it might be quite a good idea to use it. For example, a small business that sells on a cash only basis and that pays cash for wages and supplies might well use a cash basis accounting system, or a combination cash/accrual system.

However, since most established businesses have at least some purchases and sales, as well as other transactions that are not a cash basis, and since for most businesses, the IRS requires that you use accrual accounting, the matching concept is used throughout the remainder of this book.

3

FINANCIAL STATEMENTS

It is not necessary to be able to prepare financial statements to understand them. However, if you have some idea how to put together financial statements (an income statement and a balance sheet), you may have the advantage of being able to analyze the information in greater depth.

The two major components in a set of financial statements are the balance sheet and the income statement. The following sections about the balance sheet and the income statement should be read and analyzed jointly. The important relationship between the two is clear when you compare the definitions of the two types of statement:

(a) The balance sheet gives a picture of the financial position of a business at a particular point in time

(b) The income statement shows the operating results of the business over a period of time

The period of time referred to for the income statement usually ends on the date of the balance sheet.

a. THE BALANCE SHEET

As was stated earlier, the balance sheet gives a picture of the financial condition of a business at a particular point in time. On the left-hand or debit side it lists the assets or resources that a business has. On the right-hand or credit side it lists liabilities (or debts of the company) and the stockholders' equity. On a balance sheet, total assets always equal total liabilities plus equity (this is the balance sheet equation discussed in chapter 2).

The assets side of the balance sheet is generally broken down into three sections: current assets, fixed or long-term assets, and other assets. The break down of assets into these sections is not for balancing reasons, but for the convenience of the firm's owners and other readers of the financial statements.

1. Current assets

Current assets are cash or items that can or will be converted into cash within a short period of time (usually a year or less).

Current assets would include items such as cash on hand, cash in the bank, marketable securities (e.g., term deposits into which temporary surplus cash has been invested), accounts receivable, inventories, and prepaid expenses (e.g., insurance, property tax, and similar items that have been paid in advance but not "used up" at the balance sheet date).

2. Fixed (long-term) assets

Fixed or long-term assets are those of a relatively permanent nature, not intended for sale, that are used in generating revenue. For example, this category of assets would include the land, building, fixtures and equipment (including automotive equipment such as delivery trucks) that are owned by the business.

These items are shown on the balance sheet at their cost. The accumulated depreciation is deducted from the cost. Accumulated depreciation is the estimated decline in value of the assets due to wear and tear, the passage of time, changed economic conditions or other factors. (Depreciation will be discussed in more detail in the next chapter.)

The difference between the asset cost figure and the accumulated depreciation is referred to as *net book value*. Net book value does not necessarily accurately reflect the current market or replacement value of the assets in question.

3. Other assets

If a business has any other assets that do not fit into either the current or fixed categories, they are included here. An example might be leasehold costs or improvements. For example, if improvements are made to a building that you are leasing, they benefit the business for the remaining life of the lease. The costs should be spread over this life.

This cost spread is much like depreciation, except that in cases such as leasehold property it is generally called amortization.

Another example would be goodwill. Goodwill is the price you pay in excess of the value of the tangible assets (land, building, equipment) when you purchase an existing business.

4. Total assets

The total of all the asset figures (current, fixed, and other) gives the total asset value, or total resources, of the business.

5. Liabilities and owners' equity

On the right-hand side of the balance sheet are the liabilities and owners' equity sections. The liabilities and equity side of the balance sheet shows how the assets have been financed, or paid for. The liability section has two parts: current liabilities and long-term liabilities.

(a) Current liabilities

Current liabilities are those debts that must be paid, or are expected to be paid, in less than a year.

Current liabilities would include such items as accounts payable (e.g., for purchases of supplies), accrued expenses (wages/salaries due to employees, payroll tax deductions, and similar items), income tax payable, and the portion of any long-term loans or mortgages that are due within the next year.

(b) Long-term liabilities

Long-term liabilities are the debts of the business that are payable more than one year after the balance sheet date. Included in this category would be mortgages and any similar long-term loans.

6. Owners' equity

In general terms, the owners' equity section of the balance sheet is the difference between the total assets and the total liabilities. It represents the equity, or the net worth, of the owner(s) of the business.

If you are operating your own business it is likely that it will be established as a limited or incorporated company. In an incorporated company the owners' equity is comprised of two main items: capital (shares) and retained earnings.

An incorported company is limited to a maximum number of shares it can issue. This limit is known as the authorized number of shares. Shares generally have a par, or stated, value. It is this par value, multiplied by the number of shares actually issued up to the authorized quantity, that gives the total value of capital on the balance sheet.

Most small businesses that operate as incorporated companies issue "common shares." However, some also issue "preferred shares." Preferred shares rank ahead of common shares, up to certain limits, as far as dividends are concerned. Preferred stockholders may have special voting rights, and they rank ahead of common stockholders if the business is liquidated.

The other part of the owners' equity section of the balance sheet is retained earnings. Retained earnings links the income statement and the balance sheet. For that reason the retained earnings part of the owners' equity section of the balance sheet is discussed below, after you have had a chance to read about the income statement.

A balance sheet is illustrated in Sample #1.

b. THE INCOME STATEMENT

The income statement shows the operating results of the business for a period of time (month, quarter, half-year, or year). Formal income statements are prepared at least once a year (this is required for income tax filing reasons, if for no other) and informal ones more frequently.

The income statement shows income from sales (revenue) less any expenses made to achieve that revenue. An income statement for a service firm (a travel agent) is illustrated in Sample #2. A similar type of income statement would be prepared for other types of service firms, such as laundries (see Sample #3), consulting firms, and repair companies.

The amount of detail concerning revenue and expenses to be shown on the income statement depends on the type and size of the business and the needs of the owner/operator for more or less information.

In a manufacturing or wholesale company, and in some types of retail firms, the income statement would include a cost of goods sold section that is deducted from revenue to produce a gross margin or gross profit figure before other expenses are deducted. The reason for this is that the cost of goods sold figure and the gross profit to sales figure (expressed as a percentage of the related sales) are important benchmarks for measuring the success of the business. Sample #4 illustrates how cost of goods sold and gross profit are presented on an income statement.

One of the major items of expense that appears on most income statements is depreciation. Since depreciation is a special kind of expense, it will be discussed separately in the next chapter.

c. RETAINED EARNINGS

Usually the balance sheet and the income statement are accompanied by a statement of retained earnings. The statement of retained earnings is the place where the net profit of the business (from the income statement) for a period of time (let us say a year) is added to the preceding year's figure of retained earnings to give the new total. In other words, the retained earnings are the accumulated net profits, less any losses, sustained by the business since it began.

SAMPLE #1
BALANCE SHEET

MASTERPIECE MANUFACTURING LTD. — Balance Sheet as at June 30, 199-

ASSETS

Current Assets

Cash		$ 28,000
Accounts receivable		43,000
Marketable Securities		10,000
Inventories		146,000
Prepaid expenses		5,000
Total current assets		$ 232,000

Fixed Assets

Land, at cost			$ 92,000
Building, at cost	$1,333,000		
Less: Accumulated depreciation	357,000	976,000	
Equipment, at cost	$ 374,000		
Less: Accumulated depreciation	275,000	99,000	
Total fixed assets			1,167,000

Other Assets

Deferred expense	6,000
Total Assets	$1,405,000

LIABILITIES & OWNERS' EQUITY

Current Liabilities

Accounts payable	$ 19,000
Accrued expenses	4,000
Income tax payable	13,000
Current portion of mortgage	27,000
Total current liabilities	$ 63,000

Long-Term Liabilities

Mortgage on building	$840,000	
Less: current portion	27,000	813,000
Total Liabilities		$ 876,000

Owners' Equity

Capital — authorized 5 000 common shares @ $100 par value; issued and outstanding 3 000 shares	$300,000	
Retained earnings	229,000	529,000
Total Liabilities & Equity		$1,405,000

19

SUNSATIONAL TRAVEL LTD.		
Income Statement for Year Ending December 31, 199-		
Operating revenues		$2,100,000
Payments to carriers and suppliers		1,900,000
Net commission income		$ 200,000
Operating expenses:		
Salaries and wages	$120,000	
Selling related costs	32,000	
Administration costs	22,000	
Rent and other	11,000	185,000
Profit before tax		$ 15,000
Income tax		6,000
Net profit		$ 9,000

The retained earnings are not necessarily represented by cash in the bank because the money may have been used for other necessary purposes such as purchasing new equipment or physically expanding the size of the building.

A completed statement of retained earnings is illustrated in Sample #5. Note how the $66 000 net profit from the income statement (Sample #4) has been transferred to the statement of retained earnings (Sample #5) and the year-end retained earnings figure of $229 000 transferred to the balance sheet (Sample #1).

IMMACULATE CLEANING COMPANY
Income Statement for Year Ending December 31, 199-

Sales:		
Laundry	$135,000	
Dry cleaning	45,000	
Repairs and sundry	10,000	$190,000
Operating expenses:		
Salaries and wages	$94,000	
Operating and supplies	22,000	
Repairs and miscellaneous	4,000	
Accounting and legal	2,000	
Advertising	2,000	
Sundry	4,000	128,000
Profit before overheads		$ 62,000
Overhead expenses:		
Rent	$12,000	
Utilities	6,000	
Insurance	3,000	
Taxes and licences	3,000	
Depreciation — equipment	10,000	34,000
Profit before tax		$ 28,000
Income tax		7,000
Net profit		$ 21,000

SAMPLE #4
INCOME STATEMENT —
MANUFACTURING BUSINESS

RISSOLE RESTAURANT Income Statement for Year Ending June 30, 199-	
Sales	$1,250,000
Cost of goods sold	450,000
Gross profit	$ 800,000
Operating expenses: (listed in detail)	668,000
Profit before income tax	$ 132,000
Income tax	66,000
Net profit	$ 66,000

SAMPLE #5
STATEMENT OF RETAINED EARNINGS

RISSOLE RESTAURANT Statement of Retained Earnings for Year Ending June 30, 199-	
Retained earnings beginning of year	$193,000
Add profit for year	66,000
	$259,000
Deduct dividends paid	30,000
Retained earnings June 30, 199-	$229,000

4

DEPRECIATION

When Billy Big purchased a new building for his business, he recorded it on his balance sheet as a long-life asset at its original cost price. In each accounting period that benefits from the use of the new building, Billy records a portion of the cost on the income statement. At the same time he deducts from the balance sheet by way of accumulated depreciation. (See chapter 3.)

This portion of cost on Billy's income statement is called depreciation. It is shown as an expense and reduces net income for that period. This immediately improves Billy's cash flow since depreciation is a non cash expense. That is, it does not require an outlay of cash at the time Billy records the depreciation expense. It simply reduces on the books the value of the related asset.

This means Billy is reducing taxable profits and saving on income tax which means he also saves cash or increases cash flow.

Most businesses, like Billy's, will claim the maximum depreciation possible for tax purposes. What is the useful life of an asset for depreciation purposes? This is a matter of opinion influenced by such factors as inadequacy, obsolescence, and economic changes. In the case of a building, useful life could be 30, 40, or 50 years or more. In the case of a piece of equipment, it could be as short as a couple of years if a new and better piece of equipment becomes available.

There are a number of different methods for calculating depreciation, such as straight-line, declining balance, and units of production.

a. STRAIGHT-LINE DEPRECIATION

The straight-line method is probably the simplest of all depreciation methods because it spreads the cost of the asset, less any estimated trade-in or scrap value, equally over each year of the life of the asset. The equation for calculating the annual amount of depreciation is:

$$\frac{\text{Cost of asset} - \text{Trade-in value}}{\text{Service life of asset in years}}$$

If Billy Big purchases a piece of equipment at an initial cost of $32,000 and with a trade-in value of $2,000 at the end of its five-year life, the annual depreciation will be:

$$\frac{\$32,000 - \$2,000}{5 \text{ years}} = \frac{\$30,000}{5} = \$6,000 \text{ per year}$$

To obtain the monthly depreciation expense, Billy would simply divide the annual rate by 12.

Under the straight-line method, with a five-year life, one-fifth (or 20%) of the cost of the asset less its trade-in value was the annual depreciation.

b. DECLINING BALANCE DEPRECIATION

Using the same facts as above under the declining balance method, the straight-line depreciation rate of 20% is doubled to 40%. This 40% is multiplied by the undepreciated balance (book value) of the asset each year to obtain the depreciation expense for that year. Under this method, any trade-in or scrap value is ignored.

In other words, in year one, the depreciation expense would be 40% x $32,000 (the cost of the asset) = $12,800. The book value of the asset is now $32,000 - $12,800 = $19,200. Year two depreciation expense is 40% x $19,200 = $7,680. If this information is set up in the form of a schedule for all five years it would appear as follows:

YEAR	ANNUAL DEPRECIATION	NET BOOK VALUE
		$32,000
1	40% × $32,000 = $12,800	19,200
2	40 × 19,200 = 7,680	11,520
3	40 × 11,520 = 4,608	6,912
4	40 × 6,912 = 2,765	4,147
5	40 × 4,147 = 1,659	2,488

The declining balance method of depreciation is sometimes referred to as an accelerated method. You will note that the depreciation expense is high in the early years and decreases as the years go by. The philosophy of this accelerated method is that in the earlier years of the life of an asset maintenance costs are low, but increase with age. Therefore, in theory, the sum of depreciation plus maintenance should be approximately the same each year.

There are also tax advantages to using accelerated depreciation. Since depreciation is higher in the early years and can be claimed as an expense, the taxable profit will be lower and income taxes reduced. Over the long run, the total tax will be the same, but, by reducing income taxes in the early years, cash flow can be increased in early years which are often critical for a new small business.

c. UNITS OF PRODUCTION DEPRECIATION

The equation for the units of production depreciation method is:

$$\frac{\text{Cost of asset} - \text{Trade in value}}{\text{Estimated units of production during life of asset}}$$

Sally Small purchased an item of equipment for $8,000. She estimates that this equipment will produce 50,000 items before it is traded in for $800 at the end of its useful life. The cost of depreciation per unit of production will be:

$$\frac{\$8,000 - \$800}{50,000} = \frac{\$ 7,200}{50,000} = \$0.144$$

Annual depreciation expense is then based on the units produced in that year. Sally assumes that 10,000 units will be produced in year one, so the annual depreciation would be 10,000 x $0.144 = $1,440. Subsequent years' depreciation would be calculated in a similar manner.

The units of production method of depreciation does have the advantage of equitably spreading total depreciation over each period of the asset's useful life. However, it does not easily allow calculation of each period's depreciation expense in advance (e.g., in budgeting, to be covered in chapter 11). Nor is it likely to give higher depreciation amounts in the early years of the asset's life which, as mentioned earlier, is useful for reducing income taxes and increasing cash flow.

d. DEPRECIATION AND INCOME TAX

Generally the Internal Revenue Service (IRS), under the Economic Recovery Tax Act of 1981, stipulates the amount of depreciation that may be claimed for tax purposes for depreciable assets purchased after 1980.

Under the Accelerated Cost Recovery System (ACRS), the useful life of an asset and its salvage value are no longer relevant. ACRS allows you to recover the cost of an asset over a specified period of time, regardless of the life of the asset.

The general guidelines categorize most assets in either a three- or a five-year period. The three-year period covers automotive vehicles and equipment used in research and development.

As long as you are in business for a full twelve months (which would be the normal situation unless your business is just starting up), it does not matter when you buy an asset during the current fiscal year. You may still claim a full year's depreciation. In other words, even if you bought an asset on the last day of your fiscal year you may still claim a full year's depreciation.

This is useful to know if you intend to buy an asset in the next year. If you buy it late in the current year, you will be able to reduce the current year's tax payable by claiming the equivalent of a full year's depreciation.

However, if you eventually sell all your assets and receive more for them than their written down or net book value, you run into a "recapture of depreciation" situation. This simply means that you now pay tax on the excess amount of depreciation you previously claimed.

For example, if you had a small delivery business with one truck that was depreciated down to $4,000, and later you sold it for $5,000, you might be liable for tax on the recaptured depreciation of $1,000.

e. WHICH DEPRECIATION METHOD SHOULD YOU USE?

The choice of depreciation method to use is sometimes a difficult decision for the small business entrepreneur. Regardless of the method selected you must remember one thing: you can never record more depreciation for an asset than the cost of that asset.

Whether the asset is depreciated by an accelerated method or not, total depreciation expense cannot exceed the investment in that asset. Generally speaking, it is wise to show on the income statement the maximum depreciation that can be claimed to minimize income tax.

This does not mean that you cannot use a different method, or different rate of depreciation, on your books. However, when you file your annual tax return, you cannot deduct on your income statement for tax reduction purposes any depreciation in excess of the allowable rates. Also, note that you can't ever claim any depreciation on land that your company owns. Land is a nondepreciable asset as far as the IRS is concerned.

Since the subject of depreciation can be quite complex, and the regulations concerning it are changed by the government from time to time, it is best to consult with your accountant in any matter concerning depreciation. This is particularly true if you are buying the assets of a business from another company and you wish to maximize the total depreciation that you can claim in future years on those purchased assets.

5

INCOME STATEMENT ANALYSIS

In an earlier chapter, you saw examples of income statements expressed in dollars. The income statement expressed in dollars can provide useful information for a small business owner/operator to monitor the progress of the business's operations, particularly if the statements are produced on a monthly basis.

a. COMMON SIZE STATEMENTS

Sometimes it is useful to convert the dollar information on income statements to "common size." Common size simply means that the dollars are converted to a percentage basis. Total sales are usually given the value of 100%, and all other items are expressed in ratio to that 100%. Sample #6 illustrates an income statement converted to a common size basis.

The net profit, expressed as a percent of sales, is calculated by dividing net profit by sales and multiplying by 100:

$$\frac{\$\ 21,000}{\$190,000} \times 100 = 11.1\%$$

Each item on the statement can be converted in the same way by dividing it by total sales and multiplying by 100.

However, an acceptable profit to sales ratio (such as that just calculated) does not mean that the income statement should not have further analysis. In chapter 6 we will have a look at some of the ways of further analyzing income statement information in conjunction with the balance sheet.

1. Comparative common size income statements

An individual income statement is often not very meaningful by itself. Two or more successive income statements compared to each other, and preferably on a common size basis are more valuable. For example, Sample #7 illustrates an income statement placed alongside the income statement for the preceding year, with each of them expressed in common size (or percentage) terms.

In this way, changes from one year to the next are more apparent. Whether you prepare your own income statements or have your accountant do this, it is invariably a good idea to compare the current period's income statement with the previous period's.

By converting dollar amounts to percentages, you make comparison a lot easier. For example, Sample #7 shows the net profit was $21,000 in year 1 and $25,000 in year 2. Total sales increased from $190,000 to $206,000.

In relative terms, has the profit gone up at a faster or slower rate than sales? This is not easy to tell by looking only at the dollar figures. But by converting the net profit to a percentage of sales we see that it has gone from 11.1% of sales in year 1 to 12.1% of sales in year 2. In other words, in the second year, we managed to obtain a larger proportion of sales as net profit, and that is desirable.

b. TREND RESULTS

Limiting an analysis to only two periods (weeks, months, or years) can be misleading if an unusual occurrence or factor distorted the results for either of the two periods. Looking at results over a greater number of periods can often be more useful in indicating the direction in which

SAMPLE #6
COMMON SIZE INCOME STATEMENT

IMMACULATE CLEANING COMPANY
Common Size Income Statement for Year Ending December 31, 199-

Sales:			
Laundry	$135,000	71.0%	
Dry cleaning	45,000	23.7	
Repairs and sundry	10,000	5.3	100.0%
Operating expenses:			
Salaries and wages	$ 94,000	49.5%	
Operating supplies	22,000	11.6	
Repairs and miscellaneous	4,000	2.1	
Accounting and legal	2,000	1.0	
Advertising	2,000	1.0	
Sundry	4,000	2.1	
	128,000		67.3
Profit before overheads	$ 62,000		32.7%
Overhead expenses:			
Rent	$ 12,000	6.3%	
Utilities	6,000	3.2	
Insurance	3,000	1.6	
Taxes and licenses	3,000	1.6	
Depreciation — equipment	10,000	5.2	
	34,000		17.9
Profit before tax	$ 28,000		14.8%
Income tax	7,000		3.7
Net profit	$ 21,000		11.1%

COMPARATIVE COMMON SIZE INCOME STATEMENTS

For Years Ending December 31, 199- and December 31, 199-

	Year 1		Year 2	
Sales:				
Laundry	$135,000	71.0%	$148,000	71.9%
Dry cleaning	45,000	23.7	47,000	22.8
Repairs and sundry	10,000	5.3	11,000	5.3
	$190,000	100%	$206,000	100.0%
Operating expenses:				
Salaries and wages	$ 94,000	49.5%	$ 99,000	48.1%
Operating supplies	22,000	11.6	24,000	11.7
Repairs and miscellaneous	4,000	2.1	5,000	2.4
Accounting and legal	2,000	1.0	2,000	1.0
Advertising	2,000	1.0	2,000	1.0
Sundry	4,000	2.1	5,000	2.4
	128,000	67.3	137,000	66.6
Profit before overheads	$ 62,000	32.7%	$ 69,000	33.4%
Overhead expenses:				
Rent	$ 12,000	6.3%	$ 14,000	6.8%
Utilities	6,000	3.2	7,000	3.4
Insurance	3,000	1.6	3,000	1.4
Taxes and licences	3,000	1.6	3,000	1.4
Depreciation — equipment	10,000	5.2	8,000	3.9
	34,000	17.9	35,000	16.9
Profit before tax	$ 28,000	14.8%	$ 34,000	16.5%
Income tax	7,000	3.7	9,000	4.4
Net profit	$ 21,000	11.1%	$ 25,000	12.1%

your business is heading. For example, consider trend results for a business for six successive months:

MONTH	SALES	CHANGE IN SALES	PERCENTAGE CHANGE
1	$25,000		
2	30,000	+ $5,000	+ 20%
3	33,000	+ 3,000	+ 10
4	35,000	+ 2,000	+ 6
5	36,000	+ 1,000	+ 3
6	36,000	0	0

In the above figures, the change in sales dollar amounts for each period is calculated by subtracting from each month's sales the sales of the preceding month. For example, in month 3:

$33,000 - $30,000 = $3,000 change in sales

The percentage change figures are calculated by dividing each period's change in sales amount by the sales of the previous period and multiplying by 100. For example, in month 3:

$$\frac{\$\ 3,000}{\$30,000} \times 100 = 10\%$$

Over a long enough period of time, trend results show the direction the business is going. In this particular case, the trend results indicate that, although business has been increasing over the past few months, it now seems to have levelled off. Has the business reached its maximum potential in sales? Trend information such as this is useful in forecasting or budgeting (as we shall see in chapter 11).

c. INDEX TRENDS

An index trend is a way of looking at trends by first converting the dollar amounts to an index. An index is calculated by assigning a value of 100 (or 100%) in period one (the base period) for each item being tabulated. The index figure for each succeeding period is calculated by dividing the dollar amount for that period by the base period dollar amount and multiplying by 100.

The sales and wages cost dollar amounts in Table #1 have each been converted to an index trend. For example, in period 2 the sales index is:

$$\frac{\$30,000}{\$25,000} \times 100 = 120$$

In period 4 the wage cost index is:

$$\frac{\$10,800}{\$7,500} \times 100 = 144$$

TABLE #1
TREND INDEX

Period	Sales	Wage Cost	Sales Index	Wage cost Index
1	$25,000	$ 7,500	100	100
2	30,000	9,200	120	123
3	33,000	10,300	132	137
4	35,000	10,800	140	144
5	36,000	11,100	144	148
6	36,000	11,200	144	149

The completed index trend results in this particular case show that the wage cost has been increasing faster than sales. Expressed another way, sales are up 44% (144 - 100) and wage cost is up 49% (149 - 100). This is normally an undesirable trend that needs investigation and possible correction.

d. ADJUSTING FOR INFLATION

When comparing operating results and analyzing trend figures, you must be aware of the effect of changing dollar values on the results. One hundred pounds (220 kilograms) of raw materials for a manufacturing company a few years ago weighed exactly the same as one hundred pounds of raw materials today; but the amount of money required to buy those one hundred pounds today is probably quite different from the amount needed a few years ago. Prices change over time. Therefore, when you compare income and expense items over a period of time, you must consider the implications of inflation.

Consider a small business with $200,000 of sales in year one and $210,000 in year two. This is a $10,000 or 5% increase in sales. But if sales prices have been increased over the year by 10% due to inflation, then the second year sales should have been at least $220,000 just to stay even.

In other words, when comparing sales for successive periods in inflationary times, you are comparing unequal values. Last year's dollar does not have the same value as this year's. But there is a method that will allow you to convert a previous period's dollars into current period dollars so that your trends can be analyzed more meaningfully.

e. THE CONSUMER PRICE INDEX

The Consumer Price Index is probably one of the most commonly used and widely understood indexes available. But many other indexes are produced by the government and other organizations. If you select the appropriate index, dollar conversion is simple. Consider the following, which shows trend results for a small business's sales for the past five years.

Tom Trendy wanted to compare the sales figures of the small business that he had owned and operated for five years. First, he wrote down all the information to give him the trend results.

YEAR	SALES	CHANGE IN SALES	PERCENTAGE CHANGE
1	$420,000	0	0
2	450,000	$30,000	7.1%
3	465,000	15,000	3.3
4	485,000	20,000	4.3
5	510,000	25,000	5.2

Tom saw that he had an increase in sales each year — generally a favorable trend. But he knew he couldn't reasonably compare $420,000 of sales in year 1 with $510,000 of sales in year 5.

By selecting an appropriate index (such as the Consumer Price Index) and adjusting all sales to comparable year 5 dollar values, Tom had a more realistic picture of the business's sales. Tom used an index that was based on the same period of time for which he wished to adjust his sales (or expenses). The index numbers were as follows:

YEAR	INDEX NUMBER
1	105
2	112
3	119
4	128
5	142

Then Tom converted the past period's (historic) dollars to current (real) dollars with the following equation:

$$\text{Historic dollars} \times \frac{\text{Index number for current period}}{\text{Index number for historic period}} = \text{Current dollars}$$

Now Tom can see the sales dollar information converted by the index numbers to express the five-year sales in terms of today's current dollars. (See Table #2.)

TABLE #2
HISTORIC SALES CONVERTED TO CURRENT DOLLARS

Year	Index	Historic Sales	Conversion Equation	= Current Dollars
1	105	$420,000 ×	142/105 =	$568,000
2	112	450,000 ×	142/112 =	571,000
3	119	465,000 ×	142/119 =	555,000
4	128	485,000 ×	142/128 =	538,000
5	142	510,000 ×	142/142 =	510,000

The resulting picture is quite different from the unadjusted historic figures. In fact, Tom's annual sales have generally declined from year 1 to year 5, which is not normally a desirable trend.

You can obtain current Consumer Price Index (CPI) information by telephoning your local U.S. Department of Commerce district office and asking them to give you the desired data from table 784 of the Statistical Abstract of the United States produced by the U.S. Department of Commerce, Bureau of the Census.

This CPI information can be obtained for the past 10 years for any of 28 major city/metropolitan areas.

If you would like a copy of the entire Statistical Abstract of the United States that contains much information that might be useful to you in your business you can obtain it from:

Superintendent of Documents
U.S. Government Printing Office
Washington, D.C. 20402
(202) 783-3238

6

BALANCE SHEET ANALYSIS

In the previous chapter we had a look at some of the ways in which income statement information can be presented and analyzed. In this chapter we will have a look at balance sheet analysis, in conjunction with some income statement information.

Harry runs a wholesale goods store and owns both the land and building. He wants to do a balance sheet analysis to see how well he is doing. Using a balance sheet and income statement (Samples #8 and #9), he can calculate a number of important factors.

a. CURRENT RATIO

The current ratio is one of the most commonly used ratios to measure a small business's liquidity or its ability to meet its short-term debts (current liabilities) without difficulty. The equation for this ratio is:

$$\frac{\text{Current assets}}{\text{Current liabilities}}$$

Using the numbers from Harry's balance sheet (Sample #8) the ratio is:

$$\frac{\$132,000}{\$108,000} = 1.22$$

The ratio shows that for every $1.00 of short-term debt (current liabilities) there is $1.22 of current assets. A rule of thumb in business is that there should be $2.00 or more of current assets for each $1.00 of current liabilities.

However, some businesses can frequently operate without difficulty with a current ratio of less than two to one.

Each business must determine what its most effective current ratio is in order to have a current ratio position that neither creates short-term liquidity problems (too low a ratio) nor sacrifices profitability for safety (too high a ratio). If the ratio is too high you have too much money tied up in working capital (current assets less current liabilities) that is not earning a profit.

b. QUICK RATIO

Since there are some not very liquid assets included in the calculation of the current ratio, bankers and other lenders frequently like to calculate the acid test ratio. Only the cash and accounts receivable make up the numerator of this ratio:

$$\frac{\text{Cash} + \text{receivables}}{\text{Current liabilities}}$$

Harry's ratio is:

$$\frac{\$85,000 + \$15,000}{\$108,000} = 0.93$$

Lenders, under normal circumstances, like to see this ratio at 1 to 1 or higher. In Harry's case it is 0.93 to 1, or less than what is normally considered an acceptable level.

c. ACCOUNTS RECEIVABLE

Many small businesses run into financial and cash flow difficulties because they lose control over their accounts receivable. There are a couple of useful ratios for assessing the receivables situation. One of these is the calculation of the accounts receivable turnover, and the other is the calculation of the number of days sales tied up in receivables.

SAMPLE #8
BALANCE SHEET

HARRY'S WHOLESALE LTD.
Balance Sheet as at December 31, 199-

ASSETS

Current assets:		
Cash	$ 15,000	
Accounts receivable	85,000	
Inventory	27,000	
Prepaid expenses	5,000	
Total current assets		$132,000
Fixed assets:		
Land	$ 61,000	
Building	882,000	
Equipment	246,000	
	$1,189,000	
Accumulated depreciation	(422,000)	
Total fixed assets		767,000
		$899,000

LIABILITIES & OWNER'S EQUITY

Current liabilities:		
Accounts payable	$ 56,000	
Accrued expenses	4,000	
Income tax payable	22,000	
Current mortgage payable	26,000	
Total current liabilities		$108,000
Long-term liability:		
Mortgage payable		487,000
Total liabilities		$595,000
Owner's equity:		
Common shares	$200,000	
Retained earnings	104,000	
Total owner's equity		304,000
		$899,000

INCOME STATEMENT

HARRY'S WHOLESALE LTD. Income Statement for Year Ending December 31, 199-	
Sales	$956,000
Cost of goods sold	521,000
Gross profit	$435,000
Operating expenses	303,000
Profit before interest	$132,000
Interest expense	52,000
Profit before income tax	$ 80,000
Income tax	40,000
Net profit	$ 40,000

1. Accounts receivable turnover
The accounts receivable turnover is calculated as follows:

Credit sales for year
_____
Accounts receivable

Harry looked at the sales on his income statement (all sales were made on a credit basis) and the accounts receivable on his balance sheet. His turnover ratio is:

$$\frac{\$956,000}{\$85,000} = 11.25 \text{ times}$$

In a typical business that succeeds in collecting payments of accounts close to a 30 day limit, an annual turnover of 12 would be acceptable. Harry is within that limit. If the turnover was much lower than 12 it would not normally be considered good.

2. Days' sales in receivables

Another way of assessing the receivables situation is to calculate the days sales outstanding in receivables. This requires two steps. First you must calculate the average daily credit sales:

$$\frac{\text{Credit sales for year}}{260}$$

The figure of 260 is used as the denominator because Harry runs a wholesale business that is open for five days a week for 52 weeks in a year. If the business were a retail one open six days a week the denominator would be 52×6 or 312. If the business were open seven days a week (e.g., a restaurant), then the denominator would be 365.

In Harry's case it is:

$$\frac{\$956,000}{260} = \$3,677 \text{ of credit sales per day}$$

The next step is to calculate the average number of days that the year-end accounts receivable figure (from the balance sheet) represents. The equation for this is:

$$\frac{\text{Accounts receivable at year-end}}{\text{Average daily credit sales}}$$

Harry's calculations are:

$$\frac{\$85,000}{\$3,677} = 23 \text{ days}$$

Note that this figure of 23 days (in Harry's case) is "working" days and would be the equivalent of about a calendar month.

Whenever the accounts receivable results indicate that the turnover rate or number of days outstanding are over

the desirable limit of, let us say, 30 calendar days, you need
to ask and answer the following typical questions:

(a) Can the business carry these overdue accounts
without impairing its cash position?

(b) Is a 30-day limit normal for our type of business?

(c) Have we been unwise in extending more than 30
days' credit to some customers?

(d) Can anything be done to encourage more prompt
payment of outstanding accounts?

(e) Would an interest charge on overdue accounts speed
up collections?

(f) Has the bad debt loss amount increased because
some customers do not pay within the normal 30-day
limit?

d. INVENTORY TURNOVER

The amount of cash tied up in inventory can, at times, lead
to serious consequences. One measure of acceptability of
inventory level is the inventory turnover calculation:

$$\frac{\text{Cost of goods sold}}{\text{Average inventory}}$$

Average inventory is normally defined as:

$$\frac{\text{Beginning of the year inventory} + \text{end of the year inventory}}{2}$$

Harry's inventory figure from his balance sheet is the
average figure. The turnover rate would then be:

$$\frac{\$521,000}{\$27,000} = 19.3 \text{ times for the year}$$

This is a little more than 1½ times a month.

You must try to determine what the normal or standard inventory turnover rate is for your particular type of business and watch for deviations of your turnover from this standard.

e. TOTAL LIABILITIES TO TOTAL EQUITY RATIO

The total assets in a business can be financed by either liabilities (debt) or equity (shares and retained earnings). The total liabilities to total equity ratio (commonly called the debt to equity ratio) illustrates the relationship between these two forms of financing. It is calculated as follows:

$$\frac{\text{Total liabilities}}{\text{Total owners' equity}}$$

Harry's figures are:

$$\frac{\$595,000}{\$304,000} = 1.96$$

This ratio tells Harry that for each $1.00 that he has invested, the creditors, or lenders, have invested $1.96. The higher the creditors' ratio, or debt to equity ratio, the higher is the risk to the creditor or lender. In such circumstances, if a business needed additional money to expand its operations, it might find it difficult to borrow the funds.

The contradiction is that while your creditors prefer not to have the debt to equity ratio too high, you will often find it more profitable to have it as high as possible. A high debt to equity ratio is known as having high leverage. Using leverage, or trading on the equity, will be discussed later in this chapter.

f. NUMBER OF TIMES INTEREST EARNED

Another measure that creditors sometimes use to measure the safety of their investment is the number of times interest is earned during a year. The equation for this is:

$$\frac{\text{Profit before interest and income tax}}{\text{Interest expense}}$$

Harry's figures are:

$$\frac{\$132,000}{\$52,000} = 2.54 \text{ times a year}$$

Generally an investor or creditor considers the investment safe if interest is earned two or more times a year.

g. NET PROFIT TO SALES RATIO

When Harry wanted to measure his profitability, he used the common measure of net profit to sales ratio:

$$\frac{\text{Net profit}}{\text{Sales}} \times 100$$

His figures are:

$$\frac{\$40,000}{\$956,000} \times 100 = 4.2\%$$

Harry saw that out of each $1.00 of sales there were 4.2 cents net profit. The net profit to sales ratio of many businesses falls in the range of 3% to 7% (however, there are exceptions to this guideline). In absolute terms these percentages may not be too meaningful, because they do not necessarily truly represent the profitability of the business.

Consider the following two cases:

	Business A	Business B
Sales	$100,000	$100,000
Net profit	5,000	10,000
Net profit to sales ratio	5%	10%

With the same sales it seems that Business B is better. Business B is making twice as much net profit, in absolute terms, as is Business A ($10,000 to $5,000). This doubling of net profit is supported by the net profit to sales ratio (10% to 5%).

If these were two similar businesses, or two branches of the same business, these figures would indicate the relative effectiveness of the management of each in controlling costs and generating a satisfactory level of profit. However, in order to determine the profitability of a small business you need to relate the net profit to the investment by calculating the return on the owners' equity or return on investment.

h. RETURN ON OWNERS' EQUITY

The equation for return on owners' equity is:

$$\frac{\text{Net profit}}{\text{Owners' equity}} \times 100$$

Harry's figures are:

$$\frac{\$40,000}{\$304,000} \times 100 = 13.2\%$$

This ratio shows the effectiveness of Harry's use of his own funds (or equity).

How high should the ratio be? This is a matter of personal opinion. If an investor could put money either into the bank at a 10% interest rate or into a business investment at only 8% with more risk involved, the bank might look like the better of the two choices. Many people feel that 15% (after tax) is a reasonable return for the owner of a small business (with all its risks) to expect.

Now we can return to the Business A and Business B situation discussed earlier. Assume that the investment in A was $40,000 and in B $80,000. The return on the investment would be:

BUSINESS A   BUSINESS B

$$\frac{\$5,000}{\$40,000} \times 100 = 12.5\% \qquad \frac{\$10,000}{\$80,000} \times 100 = 12.5\%$$

Despite the wide difference in net profit and in net profit to sales ratio (calculated earlier), there is no difference between the two businesses as far as profitability is concerned. They are both equally as good, each yielding a 12.5% return on the investment, or return on owners' equity.

i. FINANCIAL LEVERAGE

Alice and Sue are business partners. They are considering leasing a new building for their business. They need $250,000 for equipment and working capital. They have the cash, so they could use all their own money for 100% equity financing, or they could use 50% of their own money and borrow 50% (debt financing) at a 10% interest rate.

Regardless of which financing method they use, sales and all operating costs will be the same. With either choice, they will have $50,000 profit before interest and taxes.

There is no interest expense with 100% equity financing. Interest will have to be paid with debt financing. However, interest expense is tax deductible.

Assuming a tax rate of 50% on taxable profit, Sample #10 shows the comparative operating results and the "return on investment" (ROI) for each of the two options.

In this situation, not only do Alice and Sue make a better ROI under a 50/50 debt/equity ratio (15% ROI versus 10%), but they still have $125,000 cash that they can invest in a second venture.

Because a 50/50 debt to equity ratio proved to be more profitable than 100% equity financing, Alice and Sue wondered if an 80/20 debt to equity ratio would be even more profitable.

In other words, what would the ROI be if they used only $50,000 of their own money and borrowed the remaining $200,000 at 10%? Sample #11 shows the result of this more highly levered situation.

Under this third option, the return on initial investment has now increased to 30%, and Alice and Sue still have $200,000 cash, enough for four more similar business ventures.

1. Advantages of leverage

The advantages of leverage are obvious: the higher the debt to equity ratio, the higher the ROI will be. However, this only holds true if profit (before interest) as a percent of debt is greater than the interest rate to be paid on the debt. For example, if the debt interest rate is 10%, the profit before interest must be more than 10% of the money borrowed (the debt) for leverage to be profitable.

2. Risks of leverage

With high debt (high leverage) there is a risk. If profit declines, the more highly levered the business is, the sooner it will be in financial difficulty.

In the 50/50 financing in Sample #10 (relatively low leverage), profit before interest and income tax could decline from $50,000 to $12,500 before net profit would be zero. In Sample #11 (relatively high leverage), profit before interest and income tax could decline from $50,000 to only $20,000.

SAMPLE #10
EFFECT OF LEVERAGE ON ROI

	100% equity	50% equity 50% debt
Total investment required	$250,000	$250,000
Debt financing at 10%		$125,000
Equity financing	$250,000	125,000
Profit before interest and tax	$ 50,000	$ 50,000
Interest expense 10% = $125,000		(12,500)
Profit before tax	$ 50,000	$ 37,500
Income tax 50%	(25,000)	(18,750)
Net profit	$ 25,000	$ 18,750
Return on partners' investment	$\dfrac{\$\ 25{,}000}{\$250{,}000} \times 100$ $= 10\%$	$\dfrac{\$\ 18{,}750}{\$125{,}000} \times 100$ $= 15\%$

SAMPLE #11
EFFECT OF HIGH LEVERAGE ON ROI

Total investment required	$250,000
Debt financing at 10%	$200,000
Equity financing	50,000
Profit before interest and tax	$ 50,000
Interest 10% = $200,000	(20,000)
Profit before tax	$ 30,000
Income tax 50%	(15,000)
Net profit	$ 15,000
Return on partners' investment	$\dfrac{\$15{,}000}{\$50{,}000} \times 100$ $= 30\%$

49

7

INTERNAL CONTROL

In a very small business, few internal controls are required since the owner/operator generally handles all the cash coming in and going out and, by being present, ensures the smooth and efficient operation of the business.

In larger businesses, one person control is not feasible. In fact, in larger businesses, it is necessary to organize operations into various departments and to draw up a plan of the organization, or an organization chart. Indeed, the organization chart becomes the foundation of a good internal control system since it establishes lines of communication and levels of authority and responsibility.

a. SYSTEM REQUIREMENTS

A good system of internal control requires the following:

   (a) Methods and procedures for the employees in the various jobs to follow to ensure they act according to your policies, achieve operational efficiency, and protect assets (such as cash and inventory) from waste, theft, or fraud

   (b) Reliable forms and reports that measure the efficiency and effectiveness of the business and provide information (usually of an accounting and financial nature) that, when analyzed, will identify problem areas

This information must be accurate and timely if it is to be useful. It must also be cost-effective; in other words, the benefits (cost savings) of an internal control system must be greater than the cost of its implementation and continuation.

Information produced must also be useful. If the information is not used, then you have wasted effort and money. In the two preceding chapters you saw how some of the information provided by the internal control/accounting system can be used to monitor the progress of the business.

b. PRINCIPLES OF INTERNAL CONTROL

1. Management attitude and supervision

Most employees are honest by nature but, because of a poor internal control system or, worse still, complete absence of controls, are sometimes tempted into dishonesty. If you don't care, why should your employees?

Control systems, by themselves, solve no problems. They do not absolutely protect your business against fraud or theft. A system of control may point out what is happening, but it is important to remember that even with a good control system, collusion (two or more employees working together for dishonest purposes) may go undetected for a long time. For this and other reasons any control system that you implement must be supervised by you or your delegate.

2. Establish responsibilities

One of the prerequisites for good internal control is a clear definition of job responsibilities. This goes beyond designing an organization chart. For example, in the case of deliveries of products or supplies to the business, who will do the receiving? Will it be a clerk/receiver, the maintenance man, or you? And once that is determined, how is receiving to be handled?

3. Written procedures

Once responsibilities have been determined, and procedures established, these procedures should be put into writing. In this way employees responsible will know what the procedures are. Written procedures are particularly important where turnover of employees is relatively high and continuous employee training to support the internal control system is required.

4. Forms and reports

Once procedures have been established and the employees given detailed written guidelines about how to perform tasks, you need to establish standards of performance. This requires designing forms and reports to provide information about all the business's operations. Properly designed forms and reports provide you with the information you need to determine if standards are being met and to make decisions that will improve the standards, increase productivity, and ultimately produce higher profits.

5. System monitoring and review

Any system of control must be monitored to ensure that it is continuing to provide the desired information. The system must therefore be flexible enough to be changed to suit different needs. If a reporting form needs to be changed, then it should be changed.

If a form becomes redundant, then it should be scrapped or be replaced by one that is more suitable. To have employees complete forms and/or reports that no one looks at is costly, and employees quickly become disillusioned when there seems to be no purpose to what they are asked to do.

One of your major responsibilities in internal control is constant review of the system. This review is necessary because the system will become obsolete as conditions change. In small businesses the review of the internal control system is the responsibility of the owner/operator. In larger businesses, particularly those with accounting or bookkeeping employees, the review responsibility is turned over to the employees in that department.

6. Rotate jobs

Finally, wherever possible, jobs should be rotated. Obviously this cannot be easily done in a small business with few employees. In a larger business employees may appreciate being moved from one job to another from time to time.

Job rotation has a number of advantages. Employees who know they are not going to be doing the same job for any length of time are less likely to be dishonest since the possibilities of collusion are reduced. Job rotation keeps employees from becoming bored from constantly carrying out the same tasks. It also builds flexibility into job assignments and gives employees a better understanding of how the various jobs relate to each other.

c. CASH RECEIPTS

Good cash handling and internal control procedures are not only important to the business owner or manager, but also to the employees involved, since a good system will show that employees have handled their responsibilities correctly and honestly.

All cash receipts should be deposited intact each day in the bank. A deposit slip stamped by the bank should be kept by the business. This is a form of receipt. If all cash received each day is deposited daily, no one who handles it will be tempted to "borrow" cash for a few days for personal use. It also ensures that no payments are made in cash on invoices. If this were allowed, a dishonest employee could make out a false invoice and collect cash for it.

Employees who handle cash (and other assets such as inventories) should be bonded. In this way losses are less likely to occur since the employees know they will have to answer to the insurance company if shortages arise.

1. Separate recordkeeping and asset control

One of the most important principles of good cash control is to separate recording information about cash from the actual control of cash.

Consider the accounts of the people or companies to whom you sell goods or services on credit. These accounts are an asset. Checks received in payment are given to the cashier who then records the payments on the accounts.

These checks, along with other cash and checks received from customers, are turned in as part of the total remittance at the end of the cashier's shift. There is nothing wrong with this procedure as long as the cashier is honest.

53

2. Lapping

A dishonest cashier could practice a procedure known as lapping.

So-so Sales Inc. owes you $150 on account. When it receives its statement at the month-end, it sends in a check for $150. Leta Liar, your cashier, does not record the payment on the account of So-so Sales Inc. Instead, she simply puts the check in the cash drawer and removes $150 in bills for personal use. Her remittance at the end of the shift will balance, but So-so Sales' account will still show an unpaid amount of $150.

When Better Sales Company, which has an account for $170, sends in its payments, Leta Liar records $150 as a payment on So-so Sales' account, puts the $170 check in the cash drawer and removes a further $20 in cash for personal use.

A few days later Best Buy Company makes a payment of $200 on its account. The cashier records $170 on Better Sales account, puts the $200 check in the cash drawer and takes out $30 more in cash.

This lapping of accounts will eventually increase to the point where Leta Liar can no longer cover a particular account and the fraud will be discovered. However, the outstanding account may be so large that the misappropriated cash cannot be recovered from the dishonest cashier.

To help prevent this type of loss, cash receiving and recording on accounts should be separate functions. Checks or cash received in the mail in payment of accounts should be deposited directly in the bank by you or a responsible employee. The employee looking after the accounts is simply given a list of account names and amounts received, and the appropriate accounts can be credited without that person handling any money. In other words, the responsibility for handling cash and recording payments on accounts is separated.

d. CASH DISBURSEMENTS

For minor disbursements that have to be handled by cash, a petty cash fund should be established. You should put enough cash into this fund to take care of about one month's transactions. The fund should be the responsibility of one person only. Payments out of it must be supported by a receipt, voucher, or memorandum explaining the purpose of the disbursement.

When the cash fund is almost used up, the supporting receipts, vouchers, and memoranda can be turned in, and the head cashier or manager can replenish the fund with cash up to the original amount. Receipts, vouchers, or memoranda turned in should be stamped "paid," or cancelled in some similar way, so that they cannot be reused.

All other disbursements should be made by check and supported by an approved invoice. All checks should be numbered in sequence. Checks should be prepared by you or another responsible person, but that other person should have no authority to sign the checks.

As checks are prepared, the related invoices should be cancelled in some way so that there is no possibility of fraud. Any checks spoiled in preparation should be voided so that they cannot be reused.

1. Bank reconciliation
One control that is necessary in a good internal system is a monthly bank reconciliation. At each month-end you should obtain a statement from your bank showing each daily deposit, the amount of each check paid, and other items added to or subtracted from the bank balance. The cancelled (paid) checks should accompany this statement.

To ensure control, the bank reconciliation should not be carried out by the person who records cash receipts or disbursements, otherwise "kiting" could occur.

Kiting occurs when a check is written or drawn on one bank account without recording it as a disbursement. The check is then deposited in a second bank account and the deposit is recorded. As a result the cash amount in the first bank is overstated (and cash can be removed) by an amount equal to the unrecorded check.

The steps in the reconciliation are:

(a) Compare and mark off on the statement the amount

of each check received back with your bank statement.

(b) Arrange your cancelled (paid) checks in number sequence.

(c) Verify the amount of each cancelled check with the amount of your check register or journal. Make a note of any outstanding checks. An outstanding check is one made out by you but not yet paid by the bank.

(d) To the bank statement balance add deposits made by you and not yet recorded by the bank and subtract any outstanding checks.

(e) Add any amounts to your bank balance figure added by the bank on its statement but not yet recorded by you, (e.g. bank interest earned on deposits) and subtract any deductions made by the bank (such as automatic payments on loans and interest or service charges).

Once these steps have been completed, the two balances should agree. If they do not, the work should be rechecked. If the figures still do not agree, errors have been made, either by the bank or on your books. These errors should be discovered and corrected.

To see how a reconciliation is carried out consider the following figures:

Bank statement balance	$4,456
Company bank balance	6,848
Deposit in transit	2,896
Outstanding checks — #355	372
#372	40
Interest earned on deposits	98
Bank service charge	6

The reconciliation would be as follows:

BANK BALANCE	YOUR BALANCE
$4,456	$6,848
2,896	98
(372)	(6)
(40)	
$6 940	$6,940

8

COST MANAGEMENT

Most of the cash from sales in a business goes toward expenses — as much as 90 cents or more of each sales dollar may be used to pay for expenses. Therefore, expense or cost management is important.

a. COMMON BUSINESS COSTS

In order to manage costs you must understand that there are many types of cost. If you can recognize the type of cost you are dealing with, you can make better decisions about it.

1. Discretionary costs

A discretionary cost is one that may, or may not, be incurred at the discretion of a particular person — usually the business owner or manager. Nonemergency maintenance would be an example. The building exterior could be painted this year, or the painting could be postponed until next year. In either case sales should not be affected. As the owner/manager you have the choice. You can use your own discretion.

2. Relevant costs

A relevant cost is one that makes a difference to a decision. For example, Rose's Retail Store is considering replacing one cash register with another. The relevant costs would be the cost of the new machine (less any trade-in on the old one), the cost of training employees on the new equipment, and any change in maintenance and stationery supply costs on the new machine.

3. Sunk costs

A sunk cost is a cost already incurred and about which nothing can be done. It cannot affect any future decisions.

For example, if Rose's Retail Store had spent $250 for its accountant to study the relative merits of different cash registers available, that $250 is a sunk cost. It cannot make any difference to the decision.

4. Fixed costs

Fixed costs are those that, over the short run (a year or less), do not change or vary with volume. Examples of these would be the salary of the business's manager, fire insurance expenses, and interest on a mortgage. Over the long run all these costs can change. But, in the short run, they would normally be fixed.

5. Variable costs

A variable cost is one that varies on a linear basis with sales. Very few costs are strictly linear, but some are. For example, rent based on sales, or the remuneration of employees who are paid solely on a commission basis, are variable costs.

6. Semifixed or semivariable costs

Most costs do not fit neatly into the fixed or variable category. Most have an element of fixed expense and an element of variable, and the variable element is not always variable directly to sales. For example, the cost of goods sold (since higher sales often result in item price cuts), labor, maintenance, and energy costs would all fall into this category.

In order to make useful decisions it is advantageous to break down these semifixed or semivariable costs into their two elements. (See chapter 9.)

7. Standard costs

A standard cost is what the cost should be for a given volume or level of sales. An example would be a $2 widget that National Widget Co. produces. If 100 are sold, the standard cost would be $200. If 500 were sold, the standard cost should be $1,000.

b. COST ANALYSIS —
WHICH PIECE OF EQUIPMENT TO BUY?

A good analysis of the type of cost you are dealing with will help in decision making in your business.

One of the problems that all managers face is that of choosing between alternatives such as what selling prices to charge, which employees to hire, and how to spend the advertising budget. One area of such decision making where a knowledge of costs is helpful is that of selecting a piece of equipment.

You have asked your accountant to research the typewriter equipment available and to recommend the two best pieces of equipment on the market. A decision will then be made by you about which of the two to use. The accountant's fee for this work is $500. This $500 is a sunk cost. It has to be paid regardless of your decision and, indeed, would have to be paid even if you decided not to purchase either piece of equipment.

The accountant reported the following information:

	BEST BUY TYPEWRITER	BETTER YET TYPEWRITER
Initial cost	$10,000	$8,000
Economic life	10 years	10 years
Trade in value	0	0
Annual depreciation	$ 1,000	$ 800
Initial training	600	1,100
Annual maintenance	300	200
Annual cost of forms	700	800
Annual wage cost	32,000	32,000

The relevant costs from this information are:

	BEST BUY TYPEWRITER	BETTER YET TYPEWRITER
Annual depreciation	$1,000	$ 800
Initial training	600	1,100
Annual maintenance	300	200
Annual cost of forms	700	800
Total year 1 cost	$2,600	$2,900

This information shows that in year 1 Best Buy is cheaper than Better Yet by $300. However, this saving is in year 1 only. You need to look ahead to see what the relevant costs are over the full economic life of the equipment.

After the first year, the initial training cost would be eliminated (i.e., it is now a sunk cost). The total cost for years 2 to 10 (nine times the annual cost) would be $18,000 for Best Buy and $16,200 for Better Yet.

To complete the calculation, add the total cost for years 2 to 10 to the cost for year 1. The total 10-year cost for Best Buy is $20,600, and for Better Yet $19,100. Despite year 1, the total 10-year cost is $1,500 less with the Better Yet typewriter.

In the final decision, out-of-pocket costs may not be the only factor to consider. A more comprehensive look at this type of investment decision is in chapter 13.

c. SHOULD YOU CLOSE IN THE OFF SEASON?

One of the uses of a break down of fixed and variable costs is to decide whether or not to close in the off season.

Mike's resort motel has the following annual income statement:

Sales	$150,000
Expenses	130,000
Net profit	$ 20,000

Mike decided to do an analysis of his sales and costs by the month. He found that for ten months he was making money and for two months he had a loss. (See Sample #12.)

Mike's analysis seems to indicate that he should close to eliminate the $10,000 loss during the two-month loss period. But, if he does, the fixed costs for the two months ($24,000) will have to be paid out of the ten months' profits, and $30,000 (10 months' net profit) less the two months' fixed costs of $24,000 will reduce his annual net profit to $6,000 from its present $20,000. If he does not want a reduction in annual net profit, he should not close.

There might be other factors, in such a situation, that need to be considered and that would reinforce the decision to stay open. For example, there could be sizeable additional close down and start up costs that would have to be included in the calculation of the cost of closing.

Also, Mike needs to consider the following:

(a) Would key employees return after an extended vacation?

(b) Is there a large enough pool of skilled labor available and willing to work on a seasonal basis only?

(c) Would there be recurring training time (and costs) at the start of each new season?

These are some of the kinds of questions that would have to be answered before any final decision to close was made.

SAMPLE #12
SALES AND COSTS ANALYSIS

Mike's Motel Sales and Costs by Season			
	10 months	2 months	Annual total
Sales	$135,000	$15,000	$150,000
Variable costs	$ 25,000	$ 1,000	$ 26,000
Fixed costs	80,000	24,000	104,000
Total costs	$105,000	$25,000	$130,000
Net profit (loss)	$ 30,000	($10,000)	$ 20,000

d. WHICH BUSINESS TO BUY

Business owners/managers have to make choices between alternatives on a day to day basis, but they also must decide, on a larger scale, about going into business, expanding an existing business, or buying a new business. The following situation involves fixed and variable costs.

Martha Makabuk has an opportunity to take over one of two similar existing businesses. The two businesses are close to each other in location, have the same type of clientele and size of operation, and the asking price is the same for each.

Each is doing $1,000,000 a year in sales, and each has a net profit of $100,000 a year. With only this information it is difficult for Martha to decide which would be the more profitable investment. She did a cost analysis to find some of the differences. (See Sample #13.)

1. Structure of costs

Although the sales and net profit are the same for each business, the structure of their costs is different, and this will affect the decision about which one could be more profitable.

Martha Makabuk is optimistic about the future. She feels that, without any change in fixed costs, she can increase annual sales in either business by 10%.

But the net profit for each of the two businesses will not increase by the same amount. Big Business' variable costs are 50%. This means that, out of each dollar of additional sales, it will have variable expenses of $0.50 and a net profit of $0.50 (fixed costs do not change).

Broad Business has variable costs of 30%, or $0.30 out of each sales dollar, leaving a net profit of $0.70 of extra sales. (Again, fixed costs do not change.)

Assuming that a 10% increase in sales would be achieved and no new fixed costs would be added, Martha recalculated the income statements of the two businesses. (See Sample #14.)

Note that Big Business' net profit has gone up by $50,000 to $150,000, but Broad Business has gone up by $70,000 to $170,000. In this situation Broad Business Co. would be the better investment.

e. HIGH OPERATING LEVERAGE

In chapter 6 we discussed the concept of high financial leverage (high debt to equity) for a business. By the same logic, a business that has high fixed costs relative to variable costs is said to have high operating leverage. From a profit point of view it will do better in times of rising sales than a business with low operating leverage (low fixed costs relative to variable costs).

A business with low fixed costs, however, will be better off when sales start to decline.

Suppose two businesses are going to have a decline in sales of 10% from the present $1,000,000 level and that there will be no change in fixed costs. Sample #15 shows that, with declining sales, Business A's net profit will be higher than Business B's.

In fact, if sales decline far enough Business B will be in financial difficulty long before Business A. If the break-even point were calculated (the break-even point is that level of sales at which there will be neither a profit nor a loss), Business A's sales could go down to $800,000, while Business B would be in difficulty at $857,000. This is illustrated in Sample # 16.

You could determine the break-even level of sales by trial and error (although this would be rather tedious), but there is a formula available for quick calculation of this level. The formula and a more in-depth discussion of fixed and variable costs and how this can be of great value in making many types of decisions will be covered in chapter 10.

SAMPLE #13
COST ANALYSIS

	Big Business Co.		Broad Business Co.	
	Dollars	Percent	Dollars	Percent
Sales	$1,000,000	100.0%	$1,000,000	100.0%
Variable costs	$ 500,000	50.0%	$ 300,000	30.0%
Fixed costs	400,000	40.0%	600,000	60.0%
Total costs	$ 900,000	90.0%	$ 900,000	90.0%
Net profit	$ 100,000	10.0%	$ 100,000	10.0%

SAMPLE #14
COST ANALYSIS WITH INCREASED SALES

	Big Business Co.		Broad Business Co.	
	Dollars	Percent	Dollars	Percent
Sales	$1,100,000	100.0%	$1,100,000	100.0%
Variable costs	$ 550,000	50.0%	$ 330,000	30.0%
Fixed costs	400,000	36.4%	600,000	54.5%
Total costs	$ 950,000	86.4%	$ 930,000	84.5%
Net profit	$ 150,000	13.6%	$ 170,000	15.5%

SAMPLE #15
COST ANALYSIS WITH DECREASED SALES

	Business A		Business B	
	Dollars	Percent	Dollars	Percent
Sales	$ 900,000	100.0%	$ 900,000	100.0%
Variable costs	$ 450,000	50.0%	$ 270,000	30.0%
Fixed costs	400,000	44.4%	600,000	66.7%
Total costs	$ 850,000	94.4%	$ 870,000	96.7%
Net profit	$ 50,000	5.6%	$ 30,000	3.3%

SAMPLE #16
COST ANALYSIS WITH BREAK-EVEN SALES

	Business A		Business B	
	Dollars	Percent	Dollars	Percent
Sales	$ 800,000	100.0%	$ 857,000	100.0%
Variable costs	$ 400,000	50.0%	$ 257,000	30.0%
Fixed costs	400,000	50.0%	600,000	70.0%
Total costs	$ 800,000	100.0%	$ 857,000	100.0%
Net profit	0	0	0	0

9

FIXED AND VARIABLE COSTS

Once costs have been broken down into their fixed and variable elements, valuable information is then available for use in decision making. Although some costs can be quickly identified as either fixed or variable, the majority fall into the semifixed or semivariable category. These will be referred to as semi costs from now on.

A number of different methods are available for breaking down these semi costs into fixed and variable. The two illustrated here are maximum/minimum methods and multipoint graph method.

a. MAXIMUM/MINIMUM METHOD

Ralph owns a repair service company dealing with retail customers. It has annual wage or labor costs of $120,000. Since the cost of labor is closely related to the number of customers the business handles, Ralph needs a month by month break down of the sales and the related wage costs for each month. (This information could be broken down by week, but there should be sufficient accuracy for all practical purposes with a monthly analysis). The monthly break down of sales and wage costs is given in Sample #17.

Note that the month of January has the word "minimum" alongside it. In January, sales and wage costs were at their lowest for the year. In contrast, August was the "maximum" month.

There are three steps in the maximum/minimum method:

(a) Deduct the minimum from the maximum figures:

	Sales	Wages
August (maximum)	$21,000	$13,200
January (minimum)	5,000	7,200
Differences	$16,000	$6,000

(b) Divide the wage difference by the sales difference:

$$\frac{\$\ 6,000}{\$16,000} = \$0.375 = \text{variable costs per \$1 of sales}$$

(c) Use the variable costs per \$1 of sales from step 2 to calculate the total fixed costs per month:

August total wages	\$13,200
variable costs:	
\$21,000 × \$0.375	7,875
Fixed wage costs	\$ 5,325

Ralph could equally well have used January (the minimum month) in step c. with no change in the result. The calculated fixed costs are \$5,325 a month or \$63,900 a year (12 x \$5,325). Ralph rounded this figure to the nearest thousand (\$64,000) for further calculations.

Now Ralph can break down his total annual wage costs into fixed and variable elements:

Total annual wages	\$120,000
Fixed costs	64,000
Variable costs	\$ 56,000

The calculation of the monthly fixed costs has been illustrated by arithmetical means. The maximum/minimum figures could equally as well have been plotted on a graph, as illustrated in Sample #18.

Ralph first plots the maximum figure as the upper right-hand point, and the minimum figure as the lower left-hand point. The two points are then joined by a solid line, and the solid line is continued by a dotted line down and to the left. The fixed costs figure is where the dotted line intersects the vertical axis.

Ralph has accurately drawn the graph, so the same monthly fixed wage costs figure of approximately \$5,300 is arrived at.

The maximum/minimum method is quick and simple. It uses only two sets of figures. Unfortunately, either one or both of these sets of figures may not be typical of the relationship between sales and costs for the year (e.g., a one-time wage bonus may have been paid during one of the months selected), thus distorting the figures. These distortions can be eliminated, as long as you are aware of them, by adjusting the raw figures.

b. MULTIPOINT GRAPH

To improve on the maximum/minimum method and remove possible distortions in individual month figures plot the cost and sales figures for each of the 12 months (or however many periods there are involved) on a multipoint graph.

Sample #19 illustrates a multipoint graph for Ralph's sales and wage costs for each of the 12 months. Sales and costs were taken from Sample #17. The graph illustrated is for two variables (sales and wages). In this case wages are given the name dependent variable and are plotted on the vertical axis. Wages are dependent on sales — they vary with sales. Sales, therefore, are the independent variable. The independent variable is plotted on the horizontal axis.

Note that in drawing such a graph the point where the vertical and horizontal axes meet is zero. The figures along each axis should then be plotted to scale from zero.

After plotting each of the 12 points, you have what is known as a scatter graph or a series of points scattered around a line that has been drawn through them. A straight line must be drawn.

There is no limit to how many straight lines could be drawn through the points. The line you want is the one that, to your eye, seems to fit best. Each person doing this exercise would probably view the line in a slightly different position, but most people with a reasonably good eye would come up with a line that, for all practical purposes, is close enough.

SAMPLE #17
MAXIMUM/MINIMUM
ANALYSIS OF SALES AND WAGES

	Sales	Wages
January (minimum)	$ 5,000	$ 7,200
February	9,000	8,000
March	14,000	9,000
April	13,000	10,700
May	13,000	12,300
June	15,000	12,000
July	21,000	13,000
August	21,000	13,200
September	15,000	11,900
October	10,000	7,600
November	10,000	7,600
December	7,000	7,500
Totals	$153,000	$120,000

SAMPLE #18
MAXIMUM/MINIMUM GRAPH

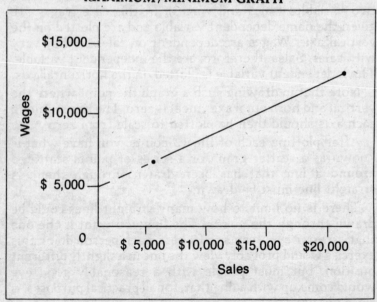

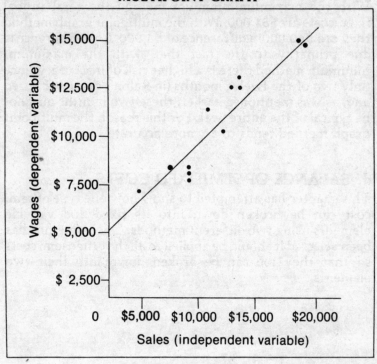

SAMPLE #19
MULTIPOINT GRAPH

The line should be drawn so that it is continued to the left until it intersects the vertical axis (the dependent variable). The intersect point reading is the fixed costs figure (wages in this case). It is $5,000 (approximately). This is the monthly figure. Converted to annual costs it is $5,000 x 12 = $60,000.

The total annual wage costs would then be broken down as follows:

Total wages	$120,000
Less fixed	60,000
Variable	$ 60,000

c. DIFFERENCE IN METHODS

With the maximum/minimum method the total annual fixed costs are $64,000. With the multipoint graph method they are $60,000; a difference of $4,000. This difference is due primarily to the fact that, with the maximum/minimum method there is a higher risk of inaccuracy since only two of the twelve months (in Ralph's case) were used and, as was mentioned earlier, these two months may not be typical of the entire year. For this reason the multipoint graph method tends to be more accurate.

d. BALANCE OF SEMIFIXED COSTS

This chapter has attempted to show how one type of semi cost can be broken down into its fixed and variable elements using two different methods. Once a method has been selected it should be applied to all the other semi costs so that they too can be broken down into their two elements.

10

COST-VOLUME-PROFIT ANALYSIS

Many questions about profit can be asked by the owner of a small business. For example:

- At what level of sales will I start losing money (i.e., what is my break-even sales level)?
- What will my net profit be at a certain level of sales?
- What is the extra sales revenue I need to cover the cost of additional advertising and still give me the profit I want?
- By how much must sales be increased to cover the cost of a wage increase and still give the profit to sales ratio I want?

These and similar questions cannot be answered simply from the traditional income statement. However, the cost-volume-profit (CVP) approach breaks down the income statement into variable and fixed costs, and then uses this information for rational decision making. Before you use this method, you must clearly understand the assumptions and limitations of CVP analysis. CVP assumes that —

(a) the costs associated with the present level of sales can be fairly accurately broken down into their fixed and variable elements (see chapter 9),

(b) fixed costs will remain fixed during the period affected by the decision being made,

(c) variable costs vary directly with sales during the period affected by the decision being made.

CVP analysis is limited to situations where economic and other conditions are assumed to be relatively stable. In highly inflationary times, for example, when it is difficult to predict sales and/or costs more than a few weeks ahead, it would be risky to use CVP for decisions too far into the future. CVP analysis is only a guide to decision making.

The CVP approach might indicate a certain decision, but other factors (such as employee or customer relations) may dictate a decision that contradicts the CVP analysis.

a. CONTRIBUTION MARGIN

Suppose you have the following annual income statement information:

INCOME STATEMENT

Sales		$306,000
Variable costs	$113,000	
Fixed costs	181,000	294,000
Profit		$ 12,000

In CVP analysis, the income statement is sometimes presented in the form of a contribution statement:

CONTRIBUTION STATEMENT

Sales	$306,000
Variable costs	113,000
Contribution to fixed costs	$193,000
Fixed costs	181,000
Profit	$ 12,000

The contribution to the fixed cost figure (in your case $193,000) is commonly referred to as the contribution margin and is simply sales less variable expenses. The profit figure does not change by presenting the fixed and variable costs in this way.

From the above information we can calculate the variable cost as a percent of sales:

$$\frac{\$113,000}{\$306,000} \times 100 = 37\%$$

74

Therefore, the contribution margin percent is 100% - 37% = 63% or 0.63.

Alternatively, it can be calculated directly by dividing it by the sales:

$$\frac{\$193,000}{\$306,000} \times 100 = 63\% \text{ or } 0.63$$

b. THE CVP EQUATION

The easiest way to use CVP analysis is to use the basic CVP equation:

$$\text{Sales level} = \frac{\text{Fixed costs} + \text{profit desired}}{\text{Contribution margin}}$$

c. ANSWERING QUESTIONS

This equation leads to the following questions, and gives the subsequent answers.

Q: At what level of sales will the business break even?

A: The level of sales at which the business will make neither a profit nor a loss (i.e., the break-even point) is:

$$\text{Sales level} = \frac{\$181,000 + 0,}{0.63} =$$

$$\$287,302, \text{ rounded to } \$287,000$$

It makes sense to round end figures when using the equation since the breakdown of fixed and variable costs may not be completely accurate in the first place. In most cases, an answer to the closest $1,000 would normally be quite acceptable.

Q: At what level of sales will I make $39,000 profit?

A: You can use the above equation for the answer, substituting $39,000 for the profit desired:

$$\text{Sales level} = \frac{\$181,000 + \$39,000}{0.63} =$$

$$\frac{\$220,000}{0.63} =$$

$$\$349,206, \text{ rounded to } \$349,000$$

Q: How much must my sales increase to cover new fixed costs?

A: Normally, if fixed costs increase and no change is made in selling prices, you would expect profits to decline by the amount of the additional fixed costs. You could then ask: by how much must sales be increased to compensate for an increase in fixed costs without reducing profit?

A simple answer would be that sales have to go up by the same amount as the fixed costs increase. But this is not correct, because to increase sales (with no increase in selling prices) you have to sell more products or service more customers. If you sell more products, your variable costs (such as wages and supplies) are going to increase.

You could arrive at a solution by trial and error, but the CVP equation used so far will solve this kind of question neatly and quickly. Simply add the old fixed costs to the new fixed costs, add the profit desired to the numerator of the equation, and divide as before by the contribution margin.

For example, suppose you wish to spend $5,000 more on advertising a year. To calculate how much more in sales you must have (assuming no price changes) to maintain your present profit level of $12,000, you would use the following figures:

$$\text{Sales level} = \frac{\$181,000 + \$5,000 + \$12,000}{0.63} =$$

$$\frac{\$198,000}{0.63} =$$

$$\$314,286, \text{ rounded to } \$314,000$$

You can easily prove the accuracy of the result (as you can with any solution to a problem using the CVP equation) as follows:

Sales		$314,000
Variable costs —		
37% x $314,000 =	$116,000	
Fixed costs	186,000	
Total costs		302,000
Profit		$ 12,000

The solution to the question tells us sales must be at the $314,000 level — an increase of $8,000 over the present sales level of $306,000.

Q: What additional sales do I need to cover a change in variable costs?

A: A change in the variable costs will change your contribution margin. Therefore the contribution margin must be recalculated, by first recalculating the variable costs percent.

Remember that your present variable costs figure of 37% was calculated by dividing total variable costs by total sales and multiplying by 100. Assume an increase in wages is to be put into effect that will increase the variable costs as a percentage of sales from 37% to 39%. The new contribution margin percent will be: 100% - 39% = 61% or 0.61. From now on, 0.61 is the denominator in the equation.

Q: What about multiple changes in the variables?

A: So far, you have considered making only one change at a time. Multiple changes can be handled in the same way without difficulty. For example, assume that $5,000 is to be spent on advertising, that the employees will be given the wage increase (changing the contribution margin to 0.61), and that the profit is to be increased from $12,000 to $20,000. The new sales level will have to be:

$$\frac{\$181,000 + \$5,000 + \$20,000}{0.61} =$$

$$\frac{\$206,000}{0.61} = 337,705 \text{ or } \$338,000$$

To prove this:

Sales		$338,000
Variable costs —		
39% x $338,000	$132,000	
Fixed costs	186,000	
		318,000
Profit		$ 20,000

Q: What about a new investment?

A: The CVP equation has been used in this chapter to illustrate how historical information from accounting records can be used to make decisions about the future. But CVP analysis is equally useful when there is no past accounting information to help you. For example, in a proposed new business, or expansion of an existing one, you simply make intelligent estimates of what the fixed and variable costs are likely to be and then project potential profits from those figures.

d. PERCENT OF CAPACITY

One valuable use of CVP analysis is calculating the percentage of capacity at which a manufacturing firm is operating.

Mel's Manufacturing Company can produce 50 units of its products a day. Mel simply has to multiply the working days times 50 units to establish what production will be if full production is maintained during a specific period (e.g., a week or a month). By comparing actual production with this capacity, a percentage of capacity can be determined.

Mel's company operates 5 days a week, times 52 weeks, or 260 days a year. As 50 units per day is its capacity, the maximum production at 100% capacity would be 13,000 units per year (50 units x 260 days). If actual production is 12,000 units, the percentage of capacity for the year would be:

$$\frac{12,000}{13,000} \times 100 = 92\%$$

You can use the basic CVP equation to answer questions relating to capacity levels. The only difference is that the contribution margin is expressed in dollars, rather than as a percentage. You will remember that contribution margin is sales less variable costs, converted to a percentage of sales. To use contribution margin in dollars, you simply need to find the average sale price of the product and deduct from it the average variable cost.

Mel's total sales for the 12,000 units produced were $120,000. The average sale price is then:

$$\frac{\$120,000}{12,000} = \$10$$

If the total variable costs at this level of sales were $22,000, the average variable costs are:

$$\frac{\$22,200}{12,000} = \$1.85$$

The contribution margin is then $10.00 less $1.85, or $8.15.

If the fixed costs of Mel's manufacturing plant were $90,000, he would then use the CVP equation to solve production questions such as the break-even capacity level:

$$\frac{\$90,000}{\$8.15} = 11,043 \text{ units}$$

This would be:

$$\frac{11,043}{13,000} \times 100 = 85\% \text{ of capacity break-even point.}$$

11

BUDGETING

Budgeting is planning. In order to be successful and to make meaningful decisions about the future, you must look ahead. One way to look ahead is to prepare budgets or forecasts.

A forecast may be very simple. It may be no more than estimating tomorrow's business in, for example, a restaurant, so that sufficient employees can be notified today that they are required to work tomorrow, and for how many hours.

On the other hand a forecast of cash flow for a proposed new business may be calculated for as far ahead as five years or more.

a. PURPOSES AND ADVANTAGES OF BUDGETING

The main purposes of budgeting are to provide:

(a) Organized estimates of such things as future sales, expenses, labor requirements, and fixture and equipment needs, broken down by time period

(b) A co-ordinated management policy, both long-term and short-term, expressed primarily in an accounting format

(c) A method of control so that actual results can be evaluated against budget plans and adjustment, if necessary, can be made

1. Advantages of budgeting

Although there are some obvious disadvantages to budgeting, such as the time and cost involved and the difficulty in predicting the future, most business people agree that the disadvantages are far outweighed by the advantages. Some of these advantages are:

(a) If key employees in the business are involved in budget preparation, it encourages motivation and improves communication. These key employees can then better identify with the business's plans and objectives.

(b) Those involved in budget preparation are required to consider alternative courses of action (e.g., what if the sales forecast does not reach the budgeted level?).

(c) Operating budgets outline in advance the sales to be achieved and the costs involved with achieving those sales. Therefore, at the end of each budget period actual results can be compared with the budget. In other words, a standard for comparison is predetermined against which actual results can be evaluated.

(d) Budgeting forces those involved to look ahead. This does not mean that what happened in the past is not important for budget preparation. However, budgets are aimed at the future and require you to consider possibilities such as price changes, increasing labor and other costs, and the competition's plans.

b. PREPARING THE BUDGET

Budgets can be either long term or short term. Long-term budgets are sometimes referred to as strategic ones and are for periods of one to five years. These budgets concern matters such as business expansion, creation of a new market, and financing. From long-term plans policies evolve concerning the day to day operations of the business, and thus the short-term budgets.

Short-term budgets could be for a day, a week, a quarter, or a year, or for any period less than a year. Short-term budgets involve using the business's resources to meet the objectives of the long-term plans.

Although there are several different types of both long-term and short-term budgets this chapter is concerned only with the operating budget for periods up to one year ahead. The operating budget is concerned with the ongoing projections of sales and expenses, or items that affect the income statement.

The budget period normally coincides with the income statement period. For example, if the company's fiscal year is the same as the calendar one, and its income statement is prepared annually at the end of the year, its budgeted income statement would be prepared in advance of that same year.

1. Who prepares the budget?

In an owner operated business, the owner would prepare the budget. The owner might just have a plan in mind about the future and operate from day to day to achieve this objective, or come as close to it as possible. If it were a formal budget, the help of an accountant might be useful in putting figures onto paper and refining them until the budget seems realistic.

In a larger business, a number of individuals (e.g., department heads) might be involved in budget preparation. These department heads might well, in turn, discuss the budget figures with employees within their own departments.

For the most part, short-term operating budgets are prepared annually with monthly projections. Each month, budgets for the remaining months of the year should be revised to adjust for any changed circumstances. Department heads should be involved in these revisions.

c. THE BUDGETED INCOME STATEMENT
1. Sales goals and objectives

The first step in preparation of the budgeted income statement is the establishment of attainable sales goals or objectives.

When you set your goals, you must be realistic. In other words, if there are any factors present that limit sales to a certain maximum level, these factors must not be ignored.

For example, a manufacturing plant cannot achieve more than a 100% capacity level. In the short run, sales can only be increased by increasing prices. But since few businesses do run at 100% year-round it would be unwise, desirable as it might be, to use 100% as the budgeted capacity on an annual basis.

Another limiting factor might be a lack of skilled labor or skilled supervisory personnel. Well-trained employees, or employees who could be trained, are often not available. Similarly, supervisory personnel who could train others are not always available.

Management policy can also be a limiting consideration. For example, in a restaurant, the manager may suggest that catering to bus tour groups would help increase sales. But if the owner feels that such groups would be too disruptive to the regular clientele, this market for increasing restaurant sales is not available.

Finally, customer demand and competition must be kept in mind when budgeting. In the short run there is a limited amount of business to go around. Increasing the capacity of a factory, or adding to the inventory of a retail clothing store, does not by itself increase the demand for the product. It takes time for demand to catch up with supply, and new businesses, or additions to existing businesses, will usually operate at a lower level of sales than desired until additional demand increases with time.

2. Preparing income statements

The starting point in the income statement budget is estimating the sales while keeping the limiting factors in mind. Although budgeted income statements are generally prepared for one year at a time, it would be helpful for any business if they were prepared monthly (with revisions, if necessary, during the budget year). Monthly income statements are necessary so that comparison with actual results can be made each month. If comparison between budget and actual were only made on a yearly basis, any required corrective action might happen 11 months too late.

How do you set about preparing a sales forecast for a small business? If you are already in business, look first at past actual sales and trends. This analysis will answer questions such as:

- For each product, how much did I sell?
- For a customer class, who am I selling to?
- For a territory, where were the products sold?
- For a market, how much did each type or class of customer buy?
- What is the past and anticipated trend of sales by product, customer, territory and/or market?

The answers to these questions can usually be found in either the sales records, or the inventory records, or both. If you can't find the answers, then your accounting records need to be changed to provide you with this information.

Electronic sales registers can often be programmed to provide this data if you first define what you want. Remember, however, not to try to program the production of too much data so that you are overwhelmed with reams of useless or overly complex information.

3. External factors
In making your sales forecast, you might also need to consider the following external factors:

- Holiday or seasonal periods
- Special events
- Population changes
- Political events
- Strikes
- Inflation and similar economic factors
- Consumer earnings
- Weather
- Fashion or style changes

- Competition
- Limiting factors

4. Internal factors

Also, there could be internal factors that you should consider, such as:

- Advertising and promotion that you plan
- Changes in policies, such as those for credit or distribution
- Product style or quality changes
- Service type or quality changes
- Price changes
- Possible inventory or production restrictions
- Working capital (see next chapter) problems
- Labor problems

Of course, it would be impossible to build all of these factors into making precise forecasts of your sales, but this list should alert you to the many factors that you must keep in mind so that you use the most critical or likely ones to refine your sales budget.

The January sales for Betty's Books Inc. for the past three years were:

1988	$30,000
1989	35,000
1990	37,000

It is now December, 1990, and Betty is completing her budget for 1991, commencing with January. The increase in sales for year 1989 over 1988 was about 17% ($5,000 ÷ $30,000). The 1990 increase over year 1989 was approximately 6%. These increases were caused entirely by increases in demand for Betty's products.

Prices have not changed in the past three years. No expansion of Betty's sales premises will occur in 1991. Because a new competitive business, Bart's Books, is being opened close by, Betty does not anticipate that sales will increase in January, but neither does she expect to lose any of her current customers. Because of economic trends, she is forced to meet rising costs by increasing prices by 10% in January, 1991. The budgeted sales for January, 1991 would therefore be: $37,000 + (10% × $37,000) = $40,700. The same type of reasoning would be applied for each of the other 11 months of 1991.

5. Deduct your operating expenses

Once forecast sales have been calculated, operating expenses that generally depend on sales (i.e., the variable costs) can be calculated and deducted.

Historic accounting records will generally show that these variable costs vary within narrow limits as a percentage of sales. The appropriate percentage of expense to sales can therefore be applied to the budgeted sales in order to calculate the dollar amount of the expense. For example, if supplies expense varies between 4-1/2% and 5-1/2% of sales, and sales are expected to be $100,000, the supplies expense for that period would be 5% x $100,000 = $5,000.

Similar calculations would be made for all other variable expenses. As you can now see, a break down of costs into their fixed and variable elements is very useful in budgeting. Once variable expenses have been calculated and deducted from sales the fixed expenses can then be deducted.

Sometimes these fixed expenses will vary at the discretion of the owner or manager. For example, you may decide that a special allocation will be added to the advertising and promotion budget during the coming year or that a particular item of expensive maintenance can be deferred for a year.

Usually these fixed expenses are estimated on an annual basis (unlike sales and variable expenses, which are generally calculated monthly). The simplest method of allocating these fixed expenses by month is to show 1/12 of the annual expense as a monthly cost.

6. Comparing your results

Comparing actual results with those planned or budgeted is probably the most important and advantageous step in the budgeting process. Comparing actual with budget allows you to examine reasons for differences. For example, if actual sales in April were $30,000 instead of the budgeted $33,000, was the difference caused by a reduction in number of customers? If so, is there an explanation? For example, are higher prices keeping customers away, or did a competitive business open nearby?

These are just some examples of the types of questions that can be asked when you analyze differences between budgeted and actual performance.

7. Corrective action

The next step in the budget process requires you to take corrective action (if this is required) because of differences between budgeted and actual figures.

The difference could be caused by an unforeseen circumstance (e.g., weather, a sudden change in economic conditions, a fire on the premises). On the other hand, a difference could be caused by failure to increase prices sufficiently to compensate for inflationary cost increases or to adjust the sales forecast to compensate for the opening of a new, nearby competitive business.

Whatever the reason, it should be corrected if possible so that future budgets can more realistically predict planned operations.

8. Improve your budget effectiveness

The final step in the budgeting process is a continual effort to try to improve the budgeting process. The information provided from past budgets, particularly the information provided by analyzing differences between actual and budgeted figures, will be helpful. By improving accuracy in budgeting, the effectiveness of your business's operation will improve.

d. BUDGETING IN A NEW BUSINESS

Owners of new businesses will find it more difficult to budget in their early years since they have no internal historic information to serve as a base. If a feasibility study has been prepared prior to opening, it could serve as a base for budgeting. Alternatively, forecasts must be founded on a combination of known facts and industry or market averages for that type and size of business.

Some of the sources of information for a new business might be:

- U.S. Department of Commerce
- Statistical Abstract of the United States (see page 37 of this book)
- Chamber of Commerce or Board of Trade
- City or Municipal Hall
- Local (federal or state) government offices
- Local business or trade associations
- Shopping center developers
- Media, such as newspapers, and radio and TV stations
- Possible competitors
- Trade publications
- Businesses in the neighborhood where you plan to locate
- Sales people
- Trade suppliers

Once you have contacted as many likely sources as possible to obtain information about possible sales levels and cost information, you can then prepare your budgeted income statement. Your first try may not be as close to actual as you would like, but once you have gone through the first actual cycle of business you can improve your budgeting effectiveness from then on by following the steps outlined in this chapter.

12

CASH MANAGEMENT

You will remember from chapter 3 that, listed under the assets, is a section called current assets. This includes items such as cash, accounts receivable, marketable securities, inventories, and prepaid expenses.

On the other side of the balance sheet is a section for the current liabilities for such items as accounts payable, accrued expenses, income tax payable, current portion of long-term mortgages, and dividends payable. The difference between total current assets and total current liabilities is known as working capital.

This chapter is about management of working capital, that is, all the accounts that appear under the "current" sections of the balance sheet. The objective is to conserve cash, earn interest on it (one possibility), and maximize profits.

Money does not always come into a business at the same rate it goes out. At times there will be excess cash on hand, at other times there will be shortages of cash. You need to anticipate both of these events so that shortages can be covered. In this way the cash balance will be kept at its optimum level.

For example, many retail sales businesses, prior to certain peak sales periods, have to borrow large amounts of money to build up their inventories, and tie up working capital, prior to the sale of the products. After the peak sale they may have surplus cash available for a few months prior to the next peak sales period. In such a situation the peaks and valleys must be fairly accurately forecast.

a. HOW MUCH WORKING CAPITAL?
How much working capital does a business need? This cannot be answered with an absolute dollar amount.

For example, suppose it were a rule of thumb that a business should have a working capital of $5,000. A business might find itself with the following:

Current assets	$15,000
Current liabilities	10,000
Working capital	$ 5,000

A larger business would have to have larger amounts of cash, inventories, accounts receivable, and other items that are current assets. Also, it would probably have larger amounts in its various current liability accounts. Its balance sheet might therefore look like this:

Current assets	$100,000
Current liabilities	95,000
Working capital	$ 5,000

The smaller business is in much better financial shape than the larger one. The former has $1.50 ($15,000 ÷ $10,000) of current assets for every $1.00 of current liabilities — a comfortable cushion. The latter has just over $1.05 ($100,000 ÷ $95,000) of current assets for each dollar of current liabilities — not so comfortable a cushion.

A general rule in business is that a company should preferably have at least $2 of current assets for each $1 of current liabilities. This would mean that its working capital ($2 - $1) is equivalent to its current liabilities.

However, this rule is primarily for companies (such as manufacturing, wholesaling, and some retailing organizations) that need to carry very large inventories that do not turn over very rapidly.

Other businesses can operate with a very low ratio of current assets to current liabilities — often as low as 1 to 1. In other words, for each $1 of current assets there is $1 of current liabilities. This means that the business has, in fact, no net working capital.

At certain times of the year, some businesses can even operate with negative working capital. In other words, current liabilities will exceed current assets. This might be typical of a business that is seasonal in nature. Such an operation would have current assets vastly in excess of current liabilities during the peak season, but the reverse situation could prevail in the off season.

Let us have a look at two of the more important working capital items that constitute cash management: cash and accounts receivable.

1. Cash

Cash on hand, as distinguished from cash in the bank, is the money in circulation in a business. This could be cash used by cashiers as "floats" or "banks" for change, petty cash, or just general cash in the safe. The amount of cash on hand should be sufficient for normal day to day operations only. Any surplus, idle cash should be deposited in the bank in savings accounts or term deposits so that it can earn interest. Preferably, each day's net cash receipts should be deposited in the bank as soon as possible the following day.

Cash in the bank in the current account should be sufficient to pay only current bills due or current payroll. Any excess funds should be invested in short-term securities or in savings or other special accounts that earn interest. Make sure you have a good balance between high interest rate and the security and liquidity of the investment.

2. Accounts receivable

Pay attention to two areas of your accounts receivable: ensure that invoices are mailed out promptly and follow up on delinquent accounts to have them collected. Money tied up in accounts receivable is money not earning a return.

Extension of credit to customers is an accepted form of business transaction, but it should not be extended to the point of allowing payments to lag two or three months behind the mailing of the invoice.

A couple of methods of keeping an eye on accounts receivable were discussed in chapter 6. Another way of keeping an eye on the accounts receivable in a business is to periodically (once a month) prepare a chart showing the age of the accounts outstanding. (See Sample #20.)

AGE	MAY 31		JUNE 30	
0-30 days	$59,000	79.5%	$56,400	74.2%
31-60 days	11,800	15.9	8,800	11.6
61-90 days	2,400	3.2	8,600	11.3
over 90 days	1,000	1.4	2,200	2.9
Totals	$74,200	100.0	$76,000	100.0

Sample #20 shows that the accounts receivable outstanding situation has not improved from May to June. In May 79.5% of total receivables were less than 30 days old. In June only 74.2% were less than 30 days outstanding. Similarly, the relative percentages in the 31-60 day category have worsened from May to June. By contrast, in the 61-90 days bracket, 11.3% of accounts receivable are outstanding in June, against only 3.2% in May.

This particular aging chart shows that the accounts receivable are getting older. If this trend continues, the business should improve its collection procedures. If, after all possible collection procedures have been explored, the account is deemed to be uncollectible (a bad debt), it would then be removed from the accounts receivable and recorded as a bad debt expense. The decision on its uncollectibility should be made by the owner or manager.

b. PROFIT IS NOT CASH

One of the most important facts you must remember in managing cash and analyzing income statements is that the net profit amount shown on the income statement is not the equivalent of cash. A reason for this is the accrual nature of the accounting process (discussed in chapter 2).

With accrual accounting, sales are recorded at the time the sale is made, even though the payment of cash for the sale might not be received until some time later. Similarly, you can purchase supplies on credit. In other words, the goods are received and used but not paid for until at least 30 days later. However, as long as the goods are used during the income statement period, they are recorded on the income statement as an expense.

Also, some expenses may be prepaid at the beginning of the year (e.g., insurance expense) yet the total insurance cost is spread equally over each monthly income statement for the entire year. This means that, for example, in January $12,000 might be paid out for annual insurance, yet only $1,000 is recorded on the January income statement as an expense, and $1,000 will be shown as an expense for each of the next 11 months.

Another complicating factor is that some items, such as depreciation, are recorded as an expense on the income statements even though no cash is involved.

If you wish to equate net income with cash (a good idea in most businesses), you must convert it to a cash basis, and one of the ways to do this is to prepare cash budgets. Cash budgets are a major aid in effective cash management.

c. CASH BUDGETS

The starting point in cash budgeting is the budgeted income statement showing the anticipated (forecast) sales and expenses by month for as long a period as is required for cash budget preparation.

In this case we will use a three month period. The budgeted income statements for the next quarter of Bee's Business are shown in Sample #21.

In order to prepare a cash budget for Bee's Business, we need some additional information.

(a) Accounting records show that, each month, approximately 60% of the sales are in the form of cash, and 40% are on credit and collected the following month.

(b) December sales were $56,000 (we need this information so that we can calculate the amount of cash that is going to be collected in January from sales made in December).

(c) Wages, supplies, utilities, and rent are paid 100% cash during each current month.

(d) Advertising has been prepaid in December ($12,000) for the entire current year. In order not to show the full $12,000 as an expense in January (since the benefit of the advertising is for a full year), the income statements show $1,000 each month for this prepaid expense.

(e) The bank balance on January 1 is $20,400.

We can now use the budgeted income statements in Sample #21 and the above information to calculate the figures for the cash budget. The process is simple. The first cash budget month is January. The cash receipts for January are:

(a) Current month sales $60,000 × 60% cash = $36,000

(b) Accounts receivable collections, December sales $56,000 × 40% = $22,400.

The cash disbursements for January are:

(a) Wages, 100% cash = $42,000

(b) Supplies, 100% cash = $3,000

(c) Utilities, 100% cash = $1,000

(d) Rent, 100% cash = $2,000

(e) Advertising was paid in December for the entire current year so the full $12,000 would have been recorded as a cash disbursement at that time. Therefore the cash amount for January = 0

(f) Depreciation does not require a disbursement of cash; it is simply a write-down of the book value of the related asset(s).

The completed cash budget for the month of January would then be as follows:

Opening bank balance	$20,400
Receipts:	
Cash sales	36,000
Collections on account	22,400
Total	$78,800

95

Disbursements:	
Wages	$42,000
Supplies	3,000
Utilities	1,000
Rent	2,000
Total	$48,000
Closing bank balance	$30,800

Note that the closing bank balance each month is calculated as: opening bank balance + receipts - disbursements = closing bank balance.

Each month the closing bank balance becomes the opening bank balance of the following month. The completed cash budget for the three-month period is shown in Sample #22. This sample shows that the bank account is expected to increase from $20,400 to $52,800 over the next three months. When the cash budget for the months of April, May, and June is prepared, it will show whether or not the bank balance is going to continue to increase or start to decline.

This sample cash budget shows that in Bee's Business there is going to be a fairly healthy surplus of cash (as long as budget projections are reasonably accurate) that should not be left to accumulate at no or low interest in a bank account. Bee might want to take $40,000 or $50,000 out of the bank account and invest it in high interest rate short-term (30-, 60-, or 90-day) securities.

Without a cash budget, Bee would not have known that she will have surplus funds on hand to use for increasing net profit and cash receipts. If the cash is taken out of the bank account and invested, the cash budget has to show this as a disbursement until the securities are cashed in and shown as a receipt.

Similarly, interest on loans, principal payments on loans, purchases of fixed assets, income tax payments, and dividend payouts are also recorded on the cash budget as disbursements. If any fixed assets are sold for cash, the cash received shows as a receipt.

SAMPLE #21
BUDGETED INCOME STATEMENT

	January	February	March
Sales	$60,000	$70,000	$80,000
Wages	$42,000	$49,000	$56,000
Supplies	3,000	3,500	4,000
Utilities	1,000	1,500	2,000
Rent	2,000	2,000	2,000
Advertising	1,000	1,000	1,000
Depreciation	4,000	4,000	4,000
	53,000	61,000	69,000
Net profit	$ 7,000	$ 9,000	$11,000

SAMPLE #22
CASH BUDGET

	January	February	March
Opening bank balance	$20,400	$30,800	$ 40,800
Receipts:			
Cash sales	36,000	42,000	48,000
Accounts receivable (collections)	22,400	24,000	28,000
	$78,800	$96,800	$116,800
Disbursements:			
Wages	$42,000	$49,000	$ 56,000
Supplies	3,000	3,500	4,000
Utilities	1,000	1,500	2,000
Rent	2,000	2,000	2,000
	$48,000	$56,000	$ 64,000
Closing bank balance	$30,800	$40,800	$ 52,800

d. NEGATIVE CASH BUDGETS

Seasonal businesses may find that for some months of the year their disbursements exceed receipts to the point that they have negative cash budgets.

However, by preparing a cash budget ahead of time, the business can show that it has anticipated the cash shortage and can plan to cover it with, for example, a short-term bank loan. Such a loan will be easier to obtain when the banker sees that good cash management is being practiced through the preparation of a cash budget.

Any loans received to cover cash shortages should be recorded as receipts on the cash budget at that time, and as disbursements when paid back.

The cash budget, particularly if prepared a year ahead, can help you not only in making decisions about investing excess funds and arranging to borrow funds to cover shortages, but also in making discretionary decisions concerning such things as major renovations, replacement of fixed assets, and payment of dividends.

13

LONG-TERM INVESTMENTS

Investment in long-term assets is sometimes referred to as capital budgeting, but we are not so much concerned in this chapter with the budgeting process as we are with the decision about whether or not to make a specific investment, or with the decision about which of two or more investments would be preferable.

The largest investment that some businesses have is in their land and building. This is a one time investment for each separate property. However, this chapter is primarily concerned about more frequent investment decisions for items such as equipment and fixtures purchase and replacement.

Long-term investment decision making differs from day to day decision making and ongoing budgeting for a number of reasons. For example, long-term investment decisions concern assets that have a relatively long life. Day to day decisions concern assets that turn over frequently. A wrong decision about a piece of equipment can have an effect for many years. A wrong decision about operating supplies has only a short-run effect.

Also, day to day operating decisions do not usually involve large amounts of money for any individual item, whereas the purchase of a long-term asset requires the outlay of a large sum of money that can have a major effect if a wrong decision is made.

Four methods of investment decision making that you can use are:

(a) Average rate of return (ARR)
(b) Payback period
(c) Net present value (NPV)
(d) Internal rate of return (IRR)

To set the scene for the average rate of return and the payback period methods, consider Wally's wholesale business, which uses a hand system for recording sales. Wally is investigating the value of installing an electronic register that will eliminate part of the present wage cost and save an estimated $4,000 a year. The register will cost $5,000 and is expected to have a five-year life with no trade-in value. Depreciation is therefore $1,000 a year ($5,000 ÷ 5). Savings and expense figures are:

Savings — employee wages	$4,000
Expenses:	
Maintenance	$ 350
Stationery	650
Depreciation	1,000
Total	$2,000
Savings before tax	$2,000
Income tax	1,000
Net annual savings	$1,000

a. AVERAGE RATE OF RETURN

The average rate of return method compares the average annual net profit (after income tax) resulting from the investment with the average investment. The formula for the average rate of return (ARR) is:

$$\frac{\text{Net annual saving}}{\text{Average investment}}$$

Note that the average investment is, simply, initial investment divided by two. Using the information from above, the ARR is:

$$\frac{\$1,000}{\$(5,000 \div 2)} \times 100 = \frac{\$1,000}{\$2,500} \times 100 = 40.0\%$$

The advantage of the average rate of return method is its simplicity. It is frequently used to compare the anticipated return from a proposal with a minimum desired return. If the proposal's return is less than desired, it is rejected. If greater than desired, a more in-depth analysis, using other investment techniques, might then be used.

The major disadvantage of the ARR is that it is based on net profit rather than on cash flow.

b. PAYBACK PERIOD

The payback period method overcomes the cash flow shortcoming of the ARR. The payback method measures the initial investment with the annual cash inflows. The equation is:

$$\frac{\text{Initial investment}}{\text{Net annual cash savings}}$$

Since the information above only gives net annual savings, and not net annual cash savings, we must first convert the net annual savings figure to a cash basis. This is done by adding back the depreciation (an expense that does not require an outlay of cash). The cash savings figure is:

Net annual savings	$1,000
Add depreciation	1,000
Net annual cash savings	$2,000

The payback period is then:

$$\frac{\$5,000}{\$2,000} = 2.5 \text{ years}$$

The payback period method, although simple, does not really measure the merits of investments, but only the speed with which the investment cost might be recovered. It has a use in evaluating a number of proposals so that only those that fall within a predetermined payback period will be considered for further evaluation using other investment techniques.

However, both the payback period and the ARR methods still suffer from a common fault: they both ignore the time value of cash flows, or the concept that money now is worth more than the same amount of money at some time in the future. This concept will be discussed in the next section, after which we will explore the use of the net present value and internal rate of return methods.

c. DISCOUNTED CASH FLOW

The concept of discounted cash flow can probably best be understood by looking first at an example of compound interest. Table #3 shows, year by year, what happens to $100.00 invested at a 10% compound interest rate. At the end of four years, the investment would be worth $146.41.

Discounting is simply the reverse of compounding interest. In other words, at a 10% interest rate, what is $146.41 four years from now worth today? The solution could be worked out manually or with a hand calculator, but can much more easily be solved by using a table of discounted cash flow factors (see Table #4).

In Table #4, look at the number, called a factor, that is opposite year 4 and under the 10% column; you will see that it is 0.6830. This factor tells us that $1 received at the end of year 4 is worth only $1 × 0.683 = $0.683 right now.

Indeed, this factor tells us, expressed in a different way, that any amount of money at the end of four years from now at a 10% interest (discount) rate is worth only 68.3% of that amount right now. You can prove this by taking the $146.41 amount at the end of year 4 from Table #3 and discounting it back to the present: $146.41 × 0.683 = $99.99803 or $100.00.

We know that $100 is the right answer because it is the amount we started with in the illustration of compounding interest in Table #3.

For a series of annual cash flows, simply apply the related annual discount factor for that year to the cash

TABLE #3
EFFECT OF COMPOUNDING INTEREST

	Jan. 1 Year 1	Dec. 31 Year 1	Dec. 31 Year 2	Dec. 31 Year 3	Dec. 31 Year 4
Balance forward Interest 10%	$100.00	$100.00 10.00	$110.00 11.00	$121.00 12.10	$133.10 13.31
Investment value end of year		$110.00	$121.00	$133.10	$146.41

TABLE #4
DISCOUNTED CASH FLOW FACTORS

Year	5%	6%	7%	8%	9%	10%	11%	12%	13%	14%	15%	16%	17%	18%	19%	20%	25%	30%
1	0.9524	0.9434	0.9346	0.9259	0.9174	0.9091	0.9009	0.8929	0.8850	0.8772	0.8696	0.8621	0.8547	0.8475	0.8403	0.8333	0.8000	0.7692
2	0.9070	0.8900	0.8734	0.8573	0.8417	0.8264	0.8116	0.7972	0.7831	0.7695	0.7561	0.7432	0.7305	0.7182	0.7062	0.6944	0.6400	0.5917
3	0.8638	0.8396	0.8163	0.7938	0.7722	0.7513	0.7312	0.7118	0.6931	0.6750	0.6575	0.6407	0.6244	0.6086	0.5934	0.5787	0.5120	0.4552
4	0.8227	0.7921	0.7629	0.7350	0.7084	0.6830	0.6587	0.6355	0.6133	0.5921	0.5718	0.5523	0.5337	0.5158	0.4987	0.4823	0.4096	0.3501
5	0.7835	0.7473	0.7130	0.6806	0.6499	0.6209	0.5935	0.5674	0.5428	0.5194	0.4972	0.4761	0.4561	0.4371	0.4191	0.4019	0.3277	0.2693
6	0.7462	0.7050	0.6663	0.6302	0.5963	0.5645	0.5346	0.5066	0.4803	0.4556	0.4323	0.4104	0.3898	0.3704	0.3521	0.3349	0.2621	0.2072
7	0.7107	0.6651	0.6228	0.5835	0.5470	0.5132	0.4817	0.4524	0.4251	0.3996	0.3759	0.3538	0.3332	0.3139	0.2959	0.2791	0.2097	0.1594
8	0.6768	0.6274	0.5820	0.5403	0.5019	0.4665	0.4339	0.4039	0.3762	0.3506	0.3269	0.3050	0.2848	0.2660	0.2487	0.2326	0.1678	0.1226
9	0.6446	0.5919	0.5439	0.5003	0.4604	0.4241	0.3909	0.3606	0.3329	0.3075	0.2843	0.2630	0.2434	0.2255	0.2090	0.1938	0.1342	0.0943
10	0.6139	0.5584	0.5084	0.4632	0.4224	0.3855	0.3522	0.3220	0.2946	0.2697	0.2472	0.2267	0.2080	0.1911	0.1756	0.1615	0.1074	0.0725
11	0.5847	0.5268	0.4751	0.4289	0.3875	0.3505	0.3173	0.2875	0.2607	0.2366	0.2149	0.1954	0.1778	0.1619	0.1476	0.1346	0.0859	0.0558
12	0.5568	0.4970	0.4440	0.3971	0.3555	0.3186	0.2858	0.2567	0.2307	0.2076	0.1869	0.1685	0.1520	0.1372	0.1240	0.1122	0.0687	0.0429
13	0.5303	0.4688	0.4150	0.3677	0.3262	0.2897	0.2575	0.2292	0.2042	0.1821	0.1625	0.1452	0.1299	0.1163	0.1042	0.0935	0.0550	0.0330
14	0.5051	0.4423	0.3878	0.3405	0.2993	0.2633	0.2320	0.2046	0.1807	0.1597	0.1413	0.1252	0.1110	0.0986	0.0876	0.0779	0.0440	0.0254
15	0.4810	0.4173	0.3625	0.3152	0.2745	0.2394	0.2090	0.1827	0.1599	0.1401	0.1229	0.1079	0.0949	0.0835	0.0736	0.0649	0.0352	0.0195
16	0.4581	0.3937	0.3387	0.2919	0.2519	0.2176	0.1883	0.1631	0.1415	0.1229	0.1069	0.0930	0.0811	0.0708	0.0618	0.0541	0.0281	0.0150
17	0.4363	0.3714	0.3166	0.2703	0.2311	0.1978	0.1696	0.1456	0.1252	0.1078	0.0929	0.0802	0.0693	0.0600	0.0520	0.0451	0.0225	0.0116
18	0.4155	0.3503	0.2959	0.2503	0.2120	0.1799	0.1528	0.1300	0.1108	0.0946	0.0808	0.0691	0.0592	0.0508	0.0437	0.0376	0.0180	0.0089
19	0.3957	0.3305	0.2765	0.2317	0.1945	0.1635	0.1377	0.1161	0.0981	0.0829	0.0703	0.0596	0.0506	0.0431	0.0367	0.0313	0.0144	0.0068
20	0.3769	0.3118	0.2584	0.2146	0.1784	0.1486	0.1240	0.1037	0.0868	0.0728	0.0611	0.0514	0.0433	0.0365	0.0308	0.0261	0.0115	0.0053

SAMPLE #23
CALCULATION OF ANNUAL NET CASH FLOWS

	Year 1	Year 2	Year 3	Year 4	Year 5
Wage saving	$4,000	$4,000	$4,000	$4,000	$4,000
Expenses:					
Training cost	$3,500				
Maintenance	400	$ 400	$ 400	$ 400	$ 400
Overhaul			400		
Stationery	600	600	600	600	600
Depreciation	800	800	800	800	800
Total	$5,300	$1,800	$2,200	$1,800	$1,800
Saving less expenses	($1,300)	$2,200	$1,800	$2,200	$2,200
Income tax 50%	0	$1,100	$ 900	1,100	1,100
Net savings	($1,300)	$1,100	$ 900	$1,100	$1,100
Add: depreciation	800	800	800	800	800
trade-in					1,000
Net cash flow	($ 500)	$1,900	$1,700	$1,900	$2,900

inflow for that year. For example, a cash inflow of $1,000 a year for each of three years using a 10% factor will produce the following total discounted cash flow:

YEAR	FACTOR	AMOUNT	TOTAL
1	0.9091	$1,000	$ 909.10
2	0.8264	$1,000	826.40
3	0.7513	$1,000	751.30
			$2,486.80

d. NET PRESENT VALUE

Discounted cash flow can be used with the net present value (NPV) method for evaluating investment proposals. Sample #23 gives projections of savings and costs for a new machine. The price of the machine is $5,000.

The estimate of the future savings and costs is the most difficult part of the exercise. In this case, you are forecasting for five years ahead. Obviously, the longer the period of time, the less accurate the estimates are likely to be. Note that depreciation is calculated as follows:

Initial cost	$5,000
Less: trade in	(1,000)
	$4,000

Depreciation (straight line) $\dfrac{\$4,000}{5}$ = $800/year

Also note that depreciation is deductible as an expense for the calculation of income tax, but this expense does not require an outlay of cash year by year. Therefore, in order to convert the annual net savings from the investment to a cash situation, the depreciation is added back each year.

Note also that there is a negative cash flow in year one. The trade-in value is a partial recovery of the initial investment and is therefore added as a positive cash flow at the end of year five. (See Sample #23.)

The initial investment and the annual net cash flow figures have been transferred to Sample #24, and, using the relevant 10% discount factors from Table #4, have been converted to a net present value basis. Note how the negative cash flow has been handled.

As you can see from Sample #24, the net present value figure is positive. It is possible for a net present value figure to be negative if the initial investment exceeds the sum of the individual years' present values. In the case of negative NPV, the investment should not be undertaken because the investment will not produce the rate of return desired.

Finally, the discount rate actually used should be realistic. It is frequently the rate that the owners expect the business to earn, after taxes, on the equity investment.

e. INTERNAL RATE OF RETURN

As we have seen, the NPV method uses a specific discount rate to determine if proposals result in a net present value greater than zero. Those that do not are rejected.

The internal rate of return (IRR) method also uses the discounted cash flow concept. However, this method determines the interest (discount) rate that will make the total discounted cash inflows equal the initial investment.

For example, Belle Businesswoman decides to investigate renting a building adjacent to her business in order to increase sales. Her investigation shows that it will cost $200,000 to renovate and equip the building. If she takes a guaranteed five-year lease, the projected cash flow (net profit after tax, with depreciation added back) for each of the five years is as follows:

YEAR	CASH FLOW
1	$ 36,000
2	40,000
3	44,000
4	50,000
5	60,000
	$230,000

In addition to the total of $230,000 cash recovery over the five years, Belle estimates the equipment can be sold for $20,000 at the end of the lease period. The total cash recovery is therefore $230,000 + $20,000 = $250,000, which is $50,000 more than the initial investment required of $200,000.

On the face of it, Belle seems to be ahead of the game. If the annual flows are discounted back to their net present value, however, a different picture emerges. (See Sample #25.) This shows that the future flows of cash discounted back to today's values using a 12% rate is less than the initial investment by over $27,000. Thus, Belle knows that, if the projections about the venture are correct, there will not be a 12% cash return on her investment.

The IRR method can be used to determine the return that will be earned if the investment is made. Belle knows that 12% is too high. By moving to a lower rate of interest, she will eventually, by trial and error, arrive at one where the NPV (the difference between total present value and initial investment) is virtually zero. This is illustrated in Sample #26 with a 7% interest (discount) rate.

The figures in Sample #26 tell Belle that the initial $200,000 investment will return the initial cash outlay except for about $300 and earn 7% on the investment. Or, stated slightly differently, Belle would recover the full $200,000 but earn slightly less than 7% interest. If she is satisfied with a 7% cash return on the investment (this is 7% after income tax), then she should go ahead with the project.

f. NON-QUANTIFIABLE BENEFITS

In this chapter various methods of making investment decisions have been examined. Information that is not easily quantifiable but that might still be relevant to decision making has been ignored. You should not forget factors like prestige, goodwill, reputation, employee or customer acceptance, and the social or environmental implications of investment decisions.

SAMPLE #24
NET PRESENT VALUE

Year	Net cash flow	Discount factor	Present value
1	($ 500)	0.9091	($ 455)
2	1,900	0.8264	1,570
3	1,700	0.7513	1,277
4	1,900	0.6830	1,298
5	2,900	0.6209	1,801
		Total present value	$5,491
		Initial investment	5,000
		Net present value	$ 491

SAMPLE #25
NET PRESENT VALUE

Year	Annual cash flow	Discount factor 12%	Present value
1	$36,000	0.8929	$32,144
2	40,000	0.7972	31,888
3	44,000	0.7118	31,319
4	50,000	0.6355	31,775
5	60,000	0.5674	34,044
5	20,000 (trade-in)	0.5674	11,348
	Total present value		$172,518
	Initial investment		200,000
	Net present value		$ 27,482)

For example, if you redecorate your reception area, you should consider the cash benefits. They may be difficult to quantify, but to retain customer goodwill the reception area may have to be redecorated.

Similarly, how do you assess the relative benefits of spending $5,000 on reception area redecoration versus Christmas bonuses for the employees? Personal judgment must come into play in such decisions.

SAMPLE #26
INTERNAL RATE OF RETURN

Year	Annual cash flow	Discount factor 7%	Present value
1	$36,000	0.9346	$ 33,646
2	40,000	0.8734	34,936
3	44,000	0.8163	35,917
4	50,000	0.7629	38,145
5	60,000	0.7130	42,780
5	20,000 (trade-in)	0.7130	4,260
	Total present value		$199,684
	Initial investment		200,000
	Net present value		($ 316)

14

LEASING

In the preceding chapter we had a look at various methods of decision making for the purchase of assets like equipment. Another method of obtaining productive assets for a business is to rent or lease.

A lease is a contractual arrangement where the owner of the asset (the lessor) grants you (the lessee) the right to the asset for a specified period of time in return for periodic lease payments. Leasing of land and/or buildings has always been a common method for an entrepreneur to minimize the investment costs of going into business. In recent years, the leasing of equipment, and similar items, has become more common.

Some suppliers of equipment will lease directly. In other cases, you can lease from a company that specializes in leasing. In other words, the lessor is a company that has bought the equipment from the supplier and has gone into the business of leasing to others.

a. ADVANTAGES OF LEASING

As a business operator there may be advantages to you to lease rather than to buy equipment and similar assets.

First, you can avoid the obsolescence that you might have if the assets are purchased outright. However, the lessor has probably considered the cost of obsolescence (a form of depreciation) and calculated it into the rental rates. However, a lease contract that allows you to replace obsolete equipment with newer equipment that comes on to the market can give you an advantage over your competitor.

Second, leasing allows you to obtain equipment that you might not be able to afford immediately or could afford only with costly financing. In other words, 100% "financing" of leased assets is possible since there is no down payment required and no loan to be repaid with interest.

Even if you have or can borrow the cash to purchase the assets you need, you may prefer to lease. Leasing allows you to use your available cash for investment in longer life assets, such as land and buildings, that over time frequently appreciate in value, whereas equipment generally depreciates.

Third, since lease payments are generally tax deductible, the lease cost is not as demanding on cash flow as it may at first appear. For example, if you lease an item of equipment for $4,000 a year that is tax deductible and your company is in a 50% tax bracket, the net cash cost of leasing is only $2,000.

	ITEM LEASED	ITEM NOT LEASED
Profit before lease cost	$10,000	$10,000
Lease expense	4,000	0
Profit before tax	$ 6,000	$10,000
Income tax 50%	3,000	5,000
Net profit	$ 3,000	$ 5,000

As you can see by these figures, even though the lease cost is $4,000, the net profit with leasing is only $2,000 less than if the item is not leased.

However, this is an oversimplified situation since, if you owned the asset, you would be able to claim depreciation on it, rather than lease expense, as a tax deduction. Also, if you borrow any money to help finance the purchase of an asset, the interest on that borrowed money is also tax deductible.

Finally, even though, with a lease the lessor is generally responsible for maintenance of the equipment while you own it, the lessor also owns any residual value in the asset at the end of the lease period. The lease contract may give you the right to purchase the asset at that time, at a specified price, or you may have the option to renew the lease for a further specified period of time.

Because of these variables, which mean that each lease arrangement can vary widely, you would be wise to obtain all necessary financial information prior to making the decision whether to buy or lease any item.

One of the ways to help you to make that decision, once you have all the facts, is to use the concept of discounted cash flow, discussed in chapter 13. This will help you narrow those facts down to a purely financial comparison.

b. A CASE STUDY

Dan's distribution company is considering the purchase for $250,000 of all the vehicles it needs. Since the company has a well established record with its bank, it can borrow the entire $250,000 required. The loan will be repayable in four equal annual installments of principal ($62,500 a year) plus interest at 8%. The vehicles will be depreciated over five years at $50,000 a year, and are assumed to have no trade-in value at the end of that period. The company is in a 50% tax bracket.

As an alternative to purchasing, the company can lease the delivery vehicles at a rental cost of $60,000 a year.

Dan's first step, with the purchase proposal, is to prepare a bank loan repayment schedule showing principal and interest payments for each of the four years of the loan. (See Sample #27.)

Next, with the purchase plan, the net cash outflow for each of the five years must be calculated, as in Sample #28. Since depreciation and the bank loan interest expense are tax deductible, and since the company is in a 50% tax bracket, there is an annual income tax savings equal to 50% of the total of those two expenses.

Thus, in year 1, the expenses of $70,000 are offset by the $35,000 tax savings. The net cost, after tax, is therefore only $35,000. This $35,000 cost has to be increased by the principal repayment on the loan of $62,500, and reduced by the depreciation expense of $50,000 (since depreciation does not require an outlay of cash).

The result is that, in year 1, the net cash outflow is $47,500. Net cash outflow figures are calculated in a similar way for the other four years.

In year 5, since the bank loan has been paid off, there is no interest and bank loan payment to be adjusted for; for this reason the net cash flow is positive (because $25,000 less is paid in income tax) rather than negative.

Sample #29 shows Dan's calculation of the annual net cash outflows under the rental option. Note that, with this option, there is no depreciation expense since the company does not own the vehicles, and no interest or principal payments since no money is to be borrowed.

Finally, Dan transfers the net cash flow figures to Sample #30 and discounts them back using the appropriate discount factor (in Dan's case 8%) from Table #4. Sample #30 shows that, from a present value point of view it would be better to rent in this particular case, since total present value of the cash outflows is lower by $8,903 ($128,681 - $119,778).

Since the decision in Dan's case favors leasing, this does not mean that the decision will always be to lease. The many variables involved can change from situation to situation. For this reason, each case must be judged on its own merits.

For example, in a purchase plan, a company might use some of its own cash as a down payment and thus borrow less from the bank. Also, under a purchase plan, there might be a trade-in value of the equipment at the end of its useful life. Further, with a lease, there might be a purchase option to the lessee at the end of the period. If the purchase option is to be exercised the additional cash outflow at that time must be considered. Finally, the terms on borrowed money can change from time to time, and different methods of depreciation can be used. For example, the use of an accelerated depreciation method will give higher depreciation expense in the earlier years, thus reducing income tax and increasing the cash flow in those years.

Because of all these and even other possibilities, each situation must be investigated on its own merits, using all the known variables in the calculations before you make your final decision.

c. SALE/LEASEBACK

A sale/leaseback arrangement can be very useful for increasing a company's cash flow. Under a sale/leaseback, an owner of a building sells the property to an investor under an agreement to lease it back for business purposes. Alternatively, the business person may own or rent the land, put up a building, and then sell both land (if owned) and building under an agreement to lease them back.

The sale/leaseback is useful for a small growing company that does not have ready access to credit on favorable terms for expansion. But, even larger companies use the sale/leaseback as a method of freeing up capital in land and/or buildings when that capital can be more effectively used to increase the return on investment via expansion, upgrading, or some other method.

Sale/leaseback can also be useful for a well established company whose building has been owned for so long that its depreciation base is now low. Selling the building may produce more than sufficient cash to compensate for recaptured depreciation and capital gain on the sale and also provide an ongoing rental expense that will help minimize the income tax burden.

There are a variety of rental arrangements possible in a sale/leaseback situation. For example, the rental could be for a fixed amount during the term of the lease. Alternatively it might be a stepped one where the rent amount increases year by year during the term of lease. The rental agreement may, or may not, allow renegotiation of this fixed or stepped amount during the life of the lease.

Another arrangement is for the rental to be a combination of a fixed amount, plus an additional amount based on a percentage of either the gross sales or net profit. This type of arrangement gives your landlord a hedge against inflation, but you can be protected by ensuring there is some maximum rent percent built into the lease contract.

Wherever there is a rent percentage based on sales, the amount to be included in sales should be clearly spelled out. For example, if the premises you are renting are subleased in part to a third party, find out if the rent you receive from that third party is to be included in the sales on which your landlord charges a percentage rent.

Some contracts call for an increasing percentage of rent as your sales increase. This can be risky for you since the accelerating percentage can seriously erode your normal profit to sales ratio as your sales increase. Wherever rent, in whole or in part, is based on your sales, your landlord is in a type of partnership arrangement with you.

In some lease contracts the variable portion of rent is based on your net profit. In that case your partnership arrangement with your landlord is more solid, since your landlord's rent depends on how successful your business is. In such cases you should be very sure that net profit is carefully defined in the contract. For example, does it allow you to deduct your salary before calculating net profit and, if yes, is there a ceiling on this salary?

Sale/leaseback is not the answer to all leasing problems, but it can have its advantages. Just remember to evaluate each case individually to determine what is best for you. If you do this, and use all the information in this book, your business and accounting problems will be lessened.

SAMPLE #27
BANK LOAN REPAYMENT SCHEDULE

Year	Interest at 8%	Principal amount	Balance
0			$250,000
1	$20,000	$62,500	187,500
2	15,000	62,500	125,000
3	10,000	62,500	62,500
4	5,000	62,500	0

SAMPLE #28
ANNUAL NET CASH OUTFLOW WITH PURCHASE

	Year 1	Year 2	Year 3	Year 4	Year 5
Interest expense (from Sample #27)	$20,000	$15,500	$10,000	$ 5,000	0
Depreciation expense	50,000	50,000	50,000	50,000	$50,000
Total tax deductible expense	$70,000	$65,000	$60,000	$55,000	$50,000
Income tax saving 50%	(35,000)	(32,500)	(30,000)	(27,500)	(25,000)
After tax cost	$35,000	$32,500	$30,000	$27,500	$25,000
Add: Principal payments	62,500	62,500	62,500	62,500	0
Deduct: depreciation	(50,000)	(50,000)	(50,000)	(50,000)	(50,000)
Net cash outflow (inflow)	$47,500	$45,000	$42,500	$40,000	($25,000)

SAMPLE #29
ANNUAL NET CASH OUTFLOW WITH RENTAL

	Year 1	Year 2	Year 3	Year 4	Year 5
Rent expense	$60,000	$60,000	$60,000	$60,000	$60,000
Income tax saving 50%	(30,000)	(30,000)	(30,000)	(30,000)	(30,000)
Net cash outflow	$30,000	$30,000	$30,000	$30,000	$30,000

SAMPLE #30
TOTAL PRESENT VALUE OF PURCHASE VERSUS RENT

Year	PURCHASE			RENT		
	Annual cash outflow (inflow)	Discount factor 8%	Present value	Annual cash outflow	Discount factor 8%	Present value
1	$47,500	0.9259	$43,980	$30,000	0.9259	$27,777
2	45,000	0.8573	38,579	30,000	0.8573	25,719
3	42,500	0.7938	33,737	30,000	0.7938	23,814
4	40,000	0.7350	29,400	30,000	0.7350	22,050
5	(25,000)	0.6806	(17,015)	30,000	0.6806	20,418
	Total present value		$128,681	Total present value		$119,778

BASIC ACCOUNTING FOR THE SMALL BUSINESS
Simple, foolproof techniques for keeping your books straight and staying out of trouble
by Clive Cornish, C.G.A.

Having bookkeeping problems? Do you feel you should know more about bookkeeping, but simply don't have time for a course? Do you wish that the paperwork in your business could be improved, but you don't know where or how to start?

This book is a down-to-earth manual on how to save your accountant's time and your time and money. Written in clear, everyday English, not in accounting jargon, this guide will help you and your office staff keep better records. $6.95

ORDER FORM

The price is subject to change without notice. Books are available in book, department, and stationery stores. If you cannot buy the book through a store, please use this order form. (Please print)

Name _____

Address _____

_____

Charge to:
❑Visa   ❑ MasterCard

Account Number _____

Validation Date_____

Expiry Date _____

Signature _____
❑**Check here for a free catalogue outlining all of our publications.**
Please send your order to:
Self-Counsel Press Inc.
1704 N. State Street
Bellingham, WA 98225

YES, please send me:
_____copies of **Basic Accounting for the Small Business** $6.95
Please add $2.50 for postage and handling.
WA residents, please add sales tax.